The Spokesman

Rojava in view

Edited by Tony Simpson

Published by Spokesman for the Bertrand Russell Peace Foundation
Ken Coates: Editor 1970 to 2010

Spokesman 135 **2017**

CONTENTS

Cartoon: with grateful thanks to Steve Bell
Cover: district market, Efrin Canton, Rojava

ISSN 1367 7748 Printed by the Russell Press Ltd., Nottingham, UK ISBN 978 0 85124 863 9

CW01648566

UK)
)
)
JK)

A CIP catalogue record for this book is available from the British Library

Published by the
Bertrand Russell Peace Foundation Ltd.,
Russell House
Bulwell Lane
Nottingham NG6 0BT
England
Tel. 0115 9784504
email:
elfeuro@compuserve.com
www.spokesmanbooks.com
www.russfound.org

Editorial Board:
John Daniels
Ken Fleet
Stuart Holland
Henry McCubbin
Nicole Morris
Abi Rhodes
Regan Scott

FSC
Mixed Sources
Product group from well-managed forests and other controlled sources

Cert no. SGS-COC-006541
www.fsc.org
© 1996 Forest Stewardship Council

...AND AT THE END OF ALL THAT YOU NOW HAVE A REAL CHOICE: TO **** OFF, OR TO DIE!!
Belltoons.co.uk - ©Steve Bell 2017 - 4098 - 8.2.17.

Editorial

Europe in view

We've heard little about European citizenship in Brexit debates, neither before the referendum of June 2016, nor since. Yet the status, rights and responsibilities of European citizenship attach to all UK nationals, whether they wish it or not. Since the early 1990s, children in the UK and other member states of the European Union are born European citizens. These millions of young people grow up able to travel freely throughout some 30 countries, study in them, in some places without paying university fees, oftentimes receiving bursaries under the Erasmus programme to encourage them to move around the Union and acquire additional language skills.

Those of us who are older became European citizens in the 1990s, in addition to our status as UK citizens or citizens of other member states. Our passports have the words 'European Union' on the front cover and, as it says inside, we are entitled to seek assistance at the embassies of other EU member states whilst travelling, should our own national embassy not be accessible.

Not only can we move freely within the territory of Member States, we also have the right as European citizens to reside in them. Millions of people take advantage of this right. More than three million UK citizens reside in other EU Member States, while more than two million EU nationals reside in the UK. Reciprocal access to health care underpins such migration, as do receipts of pensions and other benefits in the country of residence.

Many UK citizens use their right as European citizens to work in other EU Member States and, correspondingly, one readily encounters German, French, Spanish, Italian, Irish, Polish, Lithuanian and all the other EU nationalities working in Nottingham, a small city in the English Midlands, which is increasingly internationally minded. As European citizens, EU nationals are entitled to vote and to stand as candidates in local and European elections in the Member State in which they reside. However, millions of EU nationals were excluded from voting in the 'Brexit' referendum of June 2016 in the UK, as were millions of UK nationals who reside elsewhere in the European Union.

Under what is called the European Citizens' Initiative, once the required million expressions of support have been gathered, Commission representatives meet the organisers to discuss in detail the legislative issues raised in the initiative. There is also an opportunity to present the initiative at a public hearing in the European Parliament. Might it be timely to launch a Citizens' Initiative on safeguarding people from being used as 'bargaining chips' in negotiations under the Treaties, such as those associated with Brexit? A draft text is attached. Many people's lives are beset with uncertainty following the advisory vote to leave. There is also great economic uncertainty.

Len McCluskey, leader of the Unite trade union, largest in the British Isles, has rightly warned of the dire threat to UK manufacturing and the wider economy posed by Brexit. Exclusion from the European Single Market and the European Customs Union will impact directly on the jobs of many people throughout the United Kingdom. Meanwhile, 20 per cent devaluation of sterling against the dollar and 15 per cent against the euro raises prices for households and businesses in the UK, and the resultant inflation will eat into personal incomes. Few people will have voted to leave the EU in the expectation that they will be poorer as a result.

But the European Union endures as a political project to keep the peace in a substantial part of the Eurasian continent. Fundamental as this is, the EU's record during recent times includes some substantial blemishes. For example, excluding Russia from negotiations about the EU's association agreement with Ukraine has ultimately resulted in continuing conflict in Eastern Ukraine, with many people killed, injured and displaced, whilst avowedly fascist formations are integrated into the Ukrainian military and police. On the constructive side, for 13 years now, the European Parliament has hosted annual conferences about the continuing plight of the stateless Kurds, under the auspices of the EU Turkey Civic Commission. Reports from the most recent of these conferences, in December 2016, will be found elsewhere in this issue of *The Spokesman*.

In May 2019 there will be direct elections to the European Parliament. Working back from that fixed date in the political calendar has given us the Brexit timetable, or so it seems. In March 2017, Mrs May is set to give notice that the United Kingdom will withdraw from the European Union under Article 50 of the Treaty on European Union (see below). She and her interlocutors have expressed the hope that negotiations will be concluded within the two-year time frame specified in Article 50, so that the UK may depart the Union in the first half of 2019, before the elections to the European Parliament. Should the timetable slip, what will happen then? And is Article 50 revocable? Once triggered, can the UK subsequently change its mind and withdraw notice to quit? This fundamental question, to which the UK government doesn't know the answer, is being tested in the Irish courts.

Tony Simpson

Article 50–Treaty on European Union (TEU) 1. Any Member State may decide to withdraw from the Union in accordance with its own constitutional requirements. 2. A Member State which decides to withdraw shall notify the European Council of its intention. In the light of the guidelines provided by the European Council, the Union shall negotiate and conclude an agreement with that State, setting out the arrangements for its withdrawal, taking account of the framework for its future relationship with the Union. That agreement shall be negotiated in accordance with Article 218(3) of the Treaty on the Functioning of the European Union. It shall be concluded on behalf of the Union by the Council, acting by a qualified majority, after obtaining the consent of the European Parliament. 3. The Treaties shall cease to apply to the State in question from the date of entry into force of the withdrawal agreement or, failing that, two years after the notification referred to in paragraph 2, unless the European Council, in agreement with the Member State concerned, unanimously decides to extend this period. 4. For the purposes of paragraphs 2 and 3, the member of the European Council or of the Council representing the withdrawing Member State shall not participate in the discussions of the European Council or Council or in decisions concerning it. A qualified majority shall be defined in accordance with Article 238(3)(b) of the Treaty on the Functioning of the European Union. 5. If a State which has withdrawn from the Union asks to rejoin, its request shall be subject to the procedure referred to in Article 49.

* * *

Bargain not with people's lives

Under the European Citizens' Initiative, one million signatures, drawn proportionately from the 28 Member States, are required for a proposal to be considered by the European Commission. We invite comments on this draft text for such an Initiative.

'To uphold the right of all Union citizens to move and reside freely within the territory of the Member States under objective conditions of freedom and dignity (Directive 2004/38/EC), and to safeguard citizens of the Union from use as bargaining chips in any negotiations under Article 50 TEU, requests the Commission submit a proposal to retain the rights of EU citizenship for all those who have already exercised their freedom of movement prior to the departure of a Member State leaving the Union, as well as for those other nationals of the departing State who wish to retain their status as citizens of the Union.'

PYD co-chairs Asya Abdullah and Salih Muslim (right) at the Party Congress, Brussels, September 2016.

Rojava in view

Salih Muslim Muhammad
Carne Ross
Jonathan Steele

In December 2016 in Brussels, the European Parliament hosted the 13th international conference on the European Union, Turkey, the Middle East and the Kurds. Sponsored by three political groups, the European United Left/Nordic Green Left (GUE-NGL), The Greens and the Socialists and Democrats, the conference attracted hundreds of participants at a time when Kurds in many places are under attack. A keynote session was the three-way interview of Salih Muslim Muhammad, the acknowledged spokesman of Rojava ('the West' in Kurdish), a part of northern Syria distinguished by sustained attempts to establish a secular society based on social economy, gender equality and grassroots democracy that may provide an alternative model for the wider region. At the time of the interview, the battle for Aleppo continued to rage.

JS: *My name is Jonathan Steele. I'm a journalist. I used to be for many years on* The Guardian. *Now I work for the website called* Middle East Eye. *But the star of our proceedings for the next hour is, of course, Salih Muslim Mohammed, the co-chair of the Democratic Union Party of Syria – the PYD – who is really the hero of the liberation movement of the Kurds of Syria. In the whole tragedy of Syria of the last five years, the only beacon of hope, the only positive benefit of this terrible war has been the emergence of a democratic, self-ruled, autonomous region in northern Syria led by our friend Salih Muslim Mohammad – and his co-chair, Asya Abdullah. She is sitting here in the front row. What we're going to do now is hear for about five minutes or so from Mr. Muslim himself directly, and then I and a friend from New York, Carne Ross, will put some questions to him.*

Carne Ross is a former British diplomat who now runs a non-profit diplomatic advisory group called Independent Diplomat. He visited Rojava in 2015, and he's written about self-government and anarchism in his most recent book, which is called The Leaderless Revolution. *But he's taking part in this discussion in a personal capacity.*

We'll talk first about the war and the latest position in Rojava. We'll talk about peace, developing some of the ideas about the peace options in Syria, and then we'll talk, obviously, about democratic federalism and the whole experience of building a newly independent Rojava in northern Syria. Let me start by asking you, Mr Muslim, to address us.

SMM: Hello to everybody – dear guests, dear friends – and dear friends who prepared this conference here. I am glad to be among you. It really is a good opportunity to talk to each other and to discuss what's going on, and even to exchange opinions about what's going on. I am glad that Mr Carne Ross joins us. Thank you, Mr. Carne Ross. And our dear colleague here, Jonathan Steele, tried to show us as a hero. Actually, we are all friends – there are no heroes here. The only hero is the Kurdish people, who struggle, who pay the price of this struggle for freedom and protecting human rights and human values in the Middle East. We believe these human values are the only thing which connect us, all of us, together – to be protected by all humanity. So, if they are doing this, they are heroes because they are protecting humanitarian values in the Middle East. At the same time, these human values are not just for the Kurdish people, they are for all humanity. I think especially for Europeans. They also had a similar struggle, maybe in past centuries, until they reached these humanitarian values. And now these humanitarian values have been challenged in the Middle East. The Kurdish people, not only the Kurdish people, but all the components over there in Rojava protect the same values. All of us come together to defend these humanitarian values.

Actually, what's going on in the Middle East is just like the story of what happened in the 20th century at the beginning. The Sykes-Picot Agreement was at the beginning of the century. They were dividing this territory between two countries, or two imperial powers. They had a victory against the Ottomans and, at that time, nation states were valued. So they divided the Middle East according to the ideal which was common at the time, and in the modern time, to establish one nation state. And then what happened? This model was not convenient for the Middle East, as it was not convenient for the reality of Europe before. So, these nation-states established in the Middle East started to fight, and started, of course, to ignore the Kurdish existence, denying the Kurdish existence or denying the other minorities, or the nations and states who were not decided. Just like Armenia – there was the Armenian Genocide, and the same for the Syriacs, and the Kurdish massacres, and the genocide against them. And until 1923 and the Treaty of Lausanne, which stabilised things a little bit, this was continuing. What we are doing now is these nation states is trying to complete what was not completed at the beginning of the twentieth century.

Now, if Mr. Erdogan or the Turkish state tries to build an Ottoman Empire again, it's the same dream they had at the beginning. And, of course, the other ones like Saudi Arabia or the Qataris or even, maybe, the

Iranians want to establish another empire. It's the same mentality. Also, the Saudi Arabians want to have territory in Syria, or they want to change the regime in Syria, because of their interests. They still have the same mentality. The subject we are discussing is democratic alternatives for the Middle East. I think, first of all, this mentality, which is one nation state, should be changed and, according to our experience and what we have in Rojava, we try to make this solution, because we believe in many, many things.

First of all, our people should be organised and we have done it a little bit, maybe not 100 per cent as we'd like. And then we tried to change the mentality to accept to live with each other. I mean, to accept pluralism. And the second thing we tried to do was – in our model we tried to establish in Rojava – is gender equality, which, in our model, we have established now. We have three components over there: the Kurdish people, the Syriacs, the Arabs. They are living together, all of them. And we have a social contract which was put together by the representatives of these components and they have agreed it as a kind of constitution for the area. Women's gender equality is valued in all of our institutions. Already, they have a co-presidential or co-chair system, which is full equality. Secularism is also in our principles, because of the diversity of our society. Especially if you are talking about the components of our society – the Syriacs are Christians, we know that; the Kurds – we have Yazidis, also Muslims, Shia, also Alawites amongst our Kurdish society. The model we have established in Rojava, we believe this model could be adopted in Syria and, maybe, in the Middle East, in future, this democratic alternative to all systems. We believe this could be valid.

This democracy should be secular, pluralistic, and have gender equality. All these specifications we have implemented in our area. It is the alternative we are looking for. But this needs, I think, a change of the mentalities a little bit, because we are talking about mentalities which can think about the Islamic State, about the Caliphate, the Emirate, whatever it is, and empires. So this mentality should be changed, and we believe this will need more struggle. Of course, our people, we have tried to do it, and we succeeded until now to protect ourselves. But the problem is still we have this fighting.

Now what happened in the area is really a very big war. It's a very, very dirty war, really. What organises our people – I mean, this model we are trying to explain – has stood until now, and that's proof that this model is the only solution that can settle things in the future, not only in Rojava, but for Syria and the Middle East. And we are continuing this struggle. We believe the European people, the European Parliament, and other nations can help us in this matter. We are suffering from many, many subjects – if we have time, we will discuss them – like these immigrants who are used by some sides to blackmail Europe, which is against our principles. Also, we would like these people to stay in their homes and not be immigrants to Europe or wherever they are. Because we need them over there. This is brutal, they are used as tools by them, and they are trying to veil many things under them. For example, they are saying we occupy another country's land to prevent connection between the Kurdish areas. This is totally wrong. They are there just to have a connection with Daesh, because they don't want Daesh to be destroyed. So, they could persuade other sides and they are not talking about the reality.

JS: *Let me continue your theme of the dirty war which is going on now in your area. The Turkish army has moved into parts of northern Syria and is now embedded in the areas to the west of Kobane and Tal Abyad where your friends in the YPG – the People's Protection Units – are deployed in two cantons of Rojava. Do you expect the Turkish army to try to move into those areas, to move east into Kobane and Tal Abyad?*

SMM: I think we should know the real goal of the Turkish mentality, what they are doing. They are trying to veil – as I mentioned – they are trying to veil everything. Still we are dealing with a mentality saying that the best Kurd is a dead Kurd. So they want to kill the Kurds everywhere. Maybe they are planning for one step, a second step, the third step. But the matter here, especially in Rojava, the matter is connecting or not connecting. Daesh and these jihadist groups did not just come from the sky. Somebody created them, somebody helped them, somebody gave them money, somebody gave them the weapons. So, there were some forces that created them. And we believe that Turkey was one of those who created these jihadist tools to be used against the Kurds. So now, if Turkey is seeing that Daesh has been defeated in Raqqa or Tal Abyad or in Manbij, so Turkish forces cannot stay there. They don't want those tools who were created by them to be destroyed. So, we consider this invasion of the north of Syria, it's not only to the Kurdish cantons in the east, just to help Daesh, to prevent this Raqqa operation. Because, as you know, there was a very successful coalition between the Syrian Democratic Forces and the international alliance against Daesh, and they were just planning to work for Rojava. In order to prevent that, or just to help Daesh, they invaded there. The Turkish invasion, with 90 tanks and maybe the air force as well, so everyone's there – the connection between them is still going on. The families of Daesh members who were evacuated from Mosul, they are coming to Raqqa and through borders. So, this is the aim. If they have opportunities, if they find there is no resistance, of course they will destroy everything, not only in Kobane. They want to destroy the other Kurdish areas, in Kobane and Serêkaniyê. Even when they say it was a mistake in 1992 and 2003 to accept this federal system in Iraq, it was our mistake. This means they think they have an opportunity to remedy their mistakes, to destroy the federation of north Iraq, also. Still I believe, I mean this, what they are saying – the best Kurd is a dead Kurd. So, you are dealing with this mentality still.

JS: *What do you expect from the United States? It's working closely with the YPG, it's co-ordinating air strikes against Daesh with the YPG, it's using special forces alongside the YPG. So the YPG is an ally of the US, the US is an ally of the YPG. But what happens if Turkey tries to move much further into Rojava? Do you think the US will protect you or are we facing the possibility of yet another historic betrayal by the US of Kurdish interests?*

SMM: For Kurdish-American relations, I mean the United States, I think what they were planning for the Middle East at the beginning and even after the first, second stage, they took no account of the Kurdish situation. And if they did take some account, they were trying just to use us. I mean, those Kurdish people – how can they be used to help their plans? What happened, actually, on the ground was the Kurds were able to stop Daesh and these jihadis using a different mentality, with a very advanced system which they have established in their area. So the world, including the United States, started to discover the Kurdish people, who they are, and what they are doing. And of course, as the Kurdish people, we were happy about that. I mean to discover us, to establish relations, to know us. And we are in one front against those brutal groups, against Daesh and the other jihadists. So, they know the reality now. But the problem with the United States is how they can change what they have agreed before. They were listening to the others about the Kurds, getting information about the Kurds from the Turkish side or from the Arabs – from the sides who were denying the Kurdish existence. But now they have a direct connection, so it's kind of discovering the Kurdish people. Of course, we are happy about that. We are trying to go further – not only fighting against Daesh and the brutal ones. Of course, we'd like to go further – policy wise, and even diplomatically – to have very close relations. I think they'll be happy when they know the Kurdish people, the reality. Not only for the Americans, but also the others, the Europeans, also. Just a few years ago they were refusing to meet the Kurdish people. And still now, some sides refuse to meet the Kurdish people's representatives in their countries or to meet them officially because we know there is a ban from some other sides – from Turkey and some others. I know they are doing all they can just to prevent a meeting, to prevent the Kurdish people from knowing other nations and having relations with them. So, we are happy about that and we expect them to know the Kurdish people better, to understand them better, because we are talking about not only the Kurdish people in Rojava, but also the 40 million Kurds in the Middle East, the fourth nation in the Middle East. So I think the Kurdish reality could be known very well.

CR: *Could you tell us a bit about how you see the diplomatic situation with Rojava right now? Sitting here in New York at the United Nations, I'm afraid the picture is generally one of isolation, exclusion from the UN process such as it is on Syria, and exclusion from the big power politics at the moment which seems to be centred around Russia which is perhaps discussing a future dispensation, a future settlement for Syria. So, could you tell us what would your message be to the international community about Rojava and what, perhaps, diplomatically you in Rojava are doing to reach out to the diplomatic community?*

SMM: As you know, the Syrian conflict started in 2011 and there was an effort from the beginning to find a solution and discussions for it. There was Geneva One and Geneva Two, and those continued for three years. The reason for those failing was because they excluded the Rojava people. I am not talking only about the Kurdish. I am talking about the Kurds, the Syriacs, and also the others sharing in this system and the structure established in Rojava. So, excluding this one meant they were not serious to find a solution for the Syrian crisis. If they are serious, they should not exclude these components. And even, as you know, there was recently this High Negotiation Committee, which was established in Riyadh. They also excluded all these components. So, if they are serious to solve it, Rojava, the Rojava system, and the structure established in Rojava, should not be excluded anymore. If they are serious about it. And I think, until now, by not inviting them, it means they are not serious about finding a solution for Syria. We are talking about a structure, a model that could be a model for all the Middle East. So it's not only for an ordinary group to be excluded or included and it wouldn't make any change. I think it's crucial if they are seeking a solution in Rojava.

For the United Nations, also, I think until now if they don't have a direction connection with Rojava, it's a problem. Because even for humanitarian aid and so on, it doesn't go fairly. You are dealing with the regime or you are dealing with the Turkish side, you are not dealing with the people. We have many non-governmental organisations, we have organisations, institutions which are established in Rojava by the Rojava people themselves. They are not dealing with them directly. Because they are saying they are illegal. By illegal, it means they should have permission from the Syrian regime or Turkey. Both of them deny the Kurdish existence and its components, even the Syriacs. So, this is the problem even with the United Nations and so. Anyway, we try to do it. Maybe, the recent resolution by the Security Council. Maybe they have made some changes to make them able to deal directly with the United Nations. I mean, to deal directly with the components, the structure in Rojava. Maybe it will ease things a little bit for the humanitarian aid and the humanitarian health. Of course, it's not enough. We have to do more and more.

JS: *It looks very likely that the Syrian Army will take over the whole of Aleppo in the next few weeks or months. How will that – if that happens – how will that change the chances of getting an end to the war? Will it make it quicker to get an end to the war, will it make it slower, what do you think?*

SMM: Actually, we don't know. All we are trying our best to do is to stop this bloodshed in Syria. To come to the negotiation table, and to see the Syrian people doing it politically, not by fighting. We don't care, but we want this fighting in Aleppo to stop. What's going on is really a big tragedy. I mean, just shelling the areas – by the Syrians, by the Russians, by maybe the Iranians, and also those groups supported by Turkey. It's a mix really. The fighting anywhere – if the regime and the Russians when they come in – we have hope for it to be stopped. I mean, this massacre going on in Aleppo to be stopped, because, as I know, everybody is involved in it. We want this tragedy in Aleppo to be stopped by any means. But the United Nations couldn't do it. And we have – as you know – a group of Kurdish people in Sheikh Maqsoud [a neighbourhood of Aleppo] and also the areas around it, which are all controlled by the Kurdish people now. We have maybe ten thousand civilians moving into this area, protected by the YPG and the YPJ [Women's Protection Units] over there. Of course, we will do our best as the Kurdish people to protect those people, those civilians. Until now, there is maybe still some shelling coming far away from the groups outside Aleppo. But the regime didn't attack them, the Kurds in this area. They didn't attack them. We hope there could be a ceasefire, be an agreement. We don't know what they are up to. But nobody – even these groups in Aleppo, or even the Syrians and supporters – they don't care about the civilians. So, there could be a ceasefire. I mean instead of the government killing each other. There could be a ceasefire, which was rejected by the Russians and China by veto, just yesterday, I think. The resolution for a ceasefire was rejected by them. What's important for us is for this bloodshed to be stopped as soon as possible.

CR: *One of the criticisms one hears a lot about Rojava, the YPG, the PYD, the Syrian Kurds is the relationship with the Assad regime. From where I sit, this looks like your relationship with the Assad regime appears to be a kind of non-aggression pact or an uneasy truce. Could you talk about your relationship with the Assad regime and talk about how you see the future of Syria if there ever is a settlement to this dreadful war?*

SMM: For the regime, we've mentioned many times that if you have your own way, your own line and you are not connected to two sides fighting each other, each side will consider you on the other side. So, this was the way, from the beginning of the Syrian revolution, we were in the revolution because we needed what the revolution was for – democracy, freedom. We needed that. We were part of this revolution. But we could not be on the side of the regime, because already we were fighting against them, struggling against them since 2004. And we didn't believe in this revolution to go from … I mean, for some other sides to come as jihadists. We had our own line, organising the people, defending ourselves. And these forces, the democratic Syrian forces – it was the YPG, YPJ, and then it became the Syrian Democratic Forces (SDF) – they are defenders, they are just defending, they are not attacking anybody anywhere. So, they defended people when they have been attacked, and we have done the same. And now, the regime forces are far away. But tomorrow, if they are able to attack our areas, of course we will defend ourselves. And we don't have any agreements with them. But we are against sending our people to Damascus to fight over there, also. Because this is not helpful. Because defending Damascus and the other areas should be the people over there in

Damascus and that area. They should defend themselves, and we are ready to help them. But Daesh is different. For Daesh now, we are with an international alliance. We have a kind of agreement with the international alliance and the Syrian Democratic Forces to liberate Raqqa because it's harming everyone. It's not only against Rojava, it's a threat for all of Syria. So, we should be fighting against them. But for the regime, as the Kurds and the components, now what we are saying is we are part of Syria. We are not going to divide Syria. That's right. And we have a project for all of Syria, which is democratic federalism for Syria. Decentralise Syria. And we are ready to discuss with everybody, including the people in Latakia. I'm not talking about the persons, because those persons don't mean anything according to the components over here – I mean, the Alawites, the Druzes and so on. The system is accepted by everybody. It's okay, we can live together, with them. Which is democratic, decentralised … the name could be federalism or something different. We can live with them all together. A decentralised, secular system for all the people, all the components can express themselves in this Syria. So, this is the kind of Syria we want. Otherwise, if they don't accept it, Syria may be divided. I'm sorry to say that, but there is no other choice. So the only choice to keep Syria together is to have a decentralised, democratic, secular Syria. There is no other way. So, anybody who accepts this system, we are ready to live with them – including the Alawites, the Druzes, the Sunnis and so on. And this is our aim, we are trying to implement it in Syria. We are struggling for it.

JS: *You mentioned the liberation of Raqqa. When do you think this will actually happen, because everybody seems to be saying that the bulk of the forces that try and liberate Raqqa have to be Arabs. You can't have a Kurdish army, the YPG, call it an army if you like, a militia, taking the lead in liberating Raqqa. There have to be Arabs doing it. The effort to bring them together with the Syrian Democratic Forces is very slow, and patchy, and not terribly successful. So, when do you think the real effort can be made to liberate Raqqa?*

SMM: For Raqqa, I would like to clarify something which isn't often mentioned. Some sides believe that we are going to Raqqa because the United States want it, or some other forces want it, they want us to fight over there and to liberate Raqqa. It's not like that. Raqqa is very important for us in Rojava, because it's the centre for Daesh and it's close to the Jazira Canton in Rojava, it's close to Kobane, and all attacks and these bombings, car bombings, the source was from Raqqa. Raqqa was central for everything. I mean, directed to Rojava, Jazira, Kobane and others. And we believe Daesh was created in part just to kill the Kurds, to attack the Kurds. So, we cannot stay comfortable in our home while beside us there is a city like Raqqa – the capital of Daesh. So, we have to do something. To do something – not occupying, or going there to put our hands on it. No, to change it. At least, there could be some friends staying there in Raqqa. So, Raqqa is important for us, as it's important for all Syria. It's important for all the international powers also to defeat Daesh. And because of that there is a kind of agreement for the Kurdish aims and for the international alliance. The military side, I mean how they will go, I don't know exactly. But it's not only tied to the Kurdish people, because as we have heard there are some stages. The first stage, they're going to surround Raqqa for a while, until they prepare people from inside Raqqa. I mean, the Raqqa inhabitants – from among the Kurdish people, from among the Arabs to the others who are living there, to prepare a force from inside Raqqa. And of course, the people outside Raqqa will be helping them. So, the first stage is just to besiege Raqqa and it's now maybe completed. And the other one depends on the international alliance and the other powers, how much really to prepare such a power that could liberate Raqqa with the help of the international alliance and the others. As I mentioned, Raqqa is not a purely Kurdish city. The majority is not Kurdish. But we would like what happens in Raqqa … to establish the same model as what happened in Manbij. In Manbij, we can see now, there is a council. A civil council from all the components – mostly, they are Arabs, Turkmen, Circassians, and Kurdish people who were living in Raqqa. And there is a civil council who are deciding for them and taking care of the people themselves. So, there is no SDF, no YPG, no YPJ. We want the same situation for Raqqa. To make the Raqqa people decide for themselves what to do. And even to be able to protect themselves. Of course, this will be for our benefit and for Raqqa – when liberated – it will benefit all Syria, also

CR: *Do you see evidence of an emerging Russian, Turkish and, perhaps, Assad regime deal to carve up the area around Aleppo and northern Syria, allowing Turkey to keep a slice of territory or control a slice of territory between the two Kurdish controlled cantons in Afrin and to the east as well? Is there evidence of some kind of negotiations between Russia and Turkey, in particular, to ensure that there is no contiguous Kurdish-controlled area along Turkey's southern border?*

SMM: This Shahba area and the place you have mentioned are witnessing big fighting right now. It's very complicated. More than that, it doesn't depend on what Turkey is going to decide or only Russia to decide. It's very, very complicated because, already, we have people and groups fighting against Turkish occupation soldiers, I mean forces. The fighting is going on and Turkey is not able to do anything against them. They are using planes against them and they are talking about 90 tanks. It's very hard fighting going on, without Syrian Democratic Forces being involved. There are local groups fighting against them. Today, yesterday and the day before they were talking about some unidentified planes hitting Turkish soldiers. They are talking about the loss of 15 soldiers. So, I think it's not so easy. Yes, at the beginning when the Turkish invasion came of some size, they kept silent because actually it was a violation of international law – to go and occupy another country's land. It's not acceptable. But nobody said anything about it, so it means they have a kind of green light from somebody – by the Russians, or even the United States. But it doesn't mean they are going to be permanent. It's not acceptable to the people living over there. The Turkish invasion and occupation, it's not acceptable. And even the Syrians, maybe they kept silent. A kind of compromise – I mean those people, go take them from Aleppo and then they'll keep silent. I think it's a temporary thing. Because even if we look at the relations between the Russian and Turkish sides. Turkey is very, very complicated. You cannot forget what's happening among them, by letter, or saying 'I apologise for it' and finish it. It's deeper than that. They have many, many problems. Even for centuries, they've had problems. It cannot be solved in one moment. And even Syria, it's very complicated. And also we have Iranians, Hezbollah – it's more complicated. It's not so easy. I think it's a kind of problem for Turkey. I don't know what will happen. It's a problem for Turkey. They invaded, but how will they come out? Because they are not supported by the local people. Again, they are fighting against them. They are against international law. So, it's a problem for Turkey.

JS: *Let me turn now to the issue of your relations with Iraqi Kurds. Unfortunately, it's not always unity amongst Kurds. And one of the tragedies at the moment is the way the Kurdistan Regional Government (KRG), especially the Kurdistan Democratic Party (KDP) and the elite in Erbil, is basically putting Rojava under siege. Preventing humanitarian aid and other things crossing the border, crossing the river Tigris, into Rojava. How do you explain it? What is going on with the KRG relationship with Rojava? And how can you improve it? Or, how can it be improved – it doesn't rely on you alone, of course.*

SMM: It's an important point, our relations with our neighbours. But I would like to clarify something – you said the relationship with Rojava and the KRG. It's not the relationship with Rojava and the KRG. It's Rojava and the KDP – the Kurdistan Democratic Party. It's only one party. As the Kurdish people, as the Kurdish nation, we have relations with all the parties – even for south Kurdistan, east Kurdistan, for Rojava. We have good relations and we are one nation, as you know. And even for the future, we have very close visions for the future of the Kurdish people. The only thing that's different is the KDP. And they are controlling the border. They are making problems with Rojava. Of course, there are some parties which are affiliated to them in Rojava. Two parties, two small parties: one of them is the KDP Syria, the other is Yekiti. They are dealing with them, supported by them and, maybe, getting agitated by them. And they are staying in Istanbul. So, this is only the problem. It's not a problem between Rojava and the KRG for sure, because we have good relations with the others. It's only a problem between the KDP and Rojava, not only the PYD, because they are trying to present it in some ways as only a problem with the PYD and KRG. It's not like that, because they even don't accept the structure established over there. They don't accept to deal with the Syriacs, deal with the Arabs living under this system, this structure over there. And this is not because of their own policies. I think it's because of their benefits and interests with Turkey. As you know, they have a kind of economic relations with Turkey, even including the oil trade. So this is proved by many sides. It is not only what we are saying. This interest is pushing them to deal in coordinating with the Turkish side. So, this is the problem really.

CR: *Leading on from that point, could you talk about the economic situation in Rojava? When I visited a year ago, I was quite shocked by the absence of economic activity, but also above all how difficult it is to get in and out of Rojava. Of course, the northern border with Turkey is sealed. But the Kurdistan Regional Government does not make it easy to enter or exit Rojava – either for people, or for humanitarian supplies. So, could you perhaps enlarge upon what is going on economically for the people of Rojava? And perhaps also say a little about the attempts to form a co-operative economy – for instance, in agriculture, but also in other enterprises?*

SMM: Regarding economic life in Rojava, as you said, the same conditions which you have witnessed are continuing. There was a war and many places are destroyed and, of course, we are under siege, under the embargo from the northern side and even the eastern side. And maybe you can find a lot of things, but they are very expensive as they are coming through Daesh areas via the black market. So, it's difficult really, but the people are used to it. Even recently, we have those displaced people from other areas, even Mosul, we have some camps over there. Aid and helping these people is a very, very small amount. It's not enough for anything. But our people are trying to manage, because there is no other way. They are preventing the aid coming in. What we have for the economy, what we have seen for our people is a kind of, let's say, a social economy. Helping each other, co-operatives between the people, especially from the agricultural side. Now we have councils for the economy established everywhere, and councils for the people, and for the cities also. We are encouraging these co-operatives because they are the only way to share things amongst the people. So they are deciding what to do, the people themselves. As you know, politically, we are depending upon this grassroots democracy, and for the economy it's the same. We are also implementing this grassroots democracy for the economy, for the decisions. We have some committees in the cantons, in Kobane, in Jazira Canton, and Aleppo, and they are making some decisions. I mean, for the economy, how to deal especially with this harvest in Afrin, in Kobane. We have a lot of agricultural production. We need to export them. We need others. So, the people – under this embargo – are trying to manage something for themselves. It's difficult, really. Maybe in the future we can solve it, or will find our friends helping us by opening some ways. Because, as you know, many cities, many villages were destroyed during this war. Maybe, 50 to 60 per cent of Kobane is destroyed. We cannot find the materials to build it. We need some gates, some ways to be open in order to help those people, even to find the opportunity for people to work, because now the people trying to escape from Rojava is mainly because of economic reasons, not safety and security. We can find hundreds of thousands of Arabs coming to the Kurdish areas, to Rojava, just because it is safe. And we find the other people just because of economic reasons, they are coming out. So, we need some advancement, some investment in this area to keep people inside and we would like our friends to be helpful on this side – to make some investments in Rojava.

JS: *Following on from that, your 'friends' – you speak diplomatically – what about the European Union governments, the government of the United States? Why aren't they putting more pressure on the KDP in Erbil to open that border and allow humanitarian aid to go in?*

SMM: We are trying to do that. We are asking everybody to mediate, to persuade them, or to make some pressure on Turkey. Because, if we are talking about Turkey, we are talking about more than 800 kilometres. Many gates could be opened and those people could get anything for rebuilding the cities, and even for investments in these areas. It could be. Why not? But, there is some Syrian politics not to do it. As I mentioned, there are political reasons for that. Of course, we are asking the Europeans, even the United Nations, the United States, and the others; not to get permission from Turkey to do something in Rojava; not to get permission from the Syrian regime to do something in Rojava. Why don't you deal directly with those people? They have their institutions. And you can see, they can come and see what we do. I think if they just dealt directly with us. I'm not talking about recognising Rojava as a different part. I am talking about to know Rojava as part of Syria, of the Syrian Revolution, of the future of Syria, or part of a democratic federal Syria. So, you can deal with us on this basis. Until now, nobody wants to deal with us, because maybe they have their benefits or interests with some other countries. Mainly, it's Turkey, or the Iranians, or the regime. They don't accept to do it.

JS: *There have been some criticisms of the level of democracy within Rojava. People like Amnesty International have said that there has been some ethnic cleansing of Arab villages in the north of Syria, in Rojava particularly. I know that historically governments in Damascus, including particularly the regime of Hafez al-Assad, the father, tried to create an Arab belt along the northern border of Syria with Turkey, brought in Arabs. But that is a matter of history: those Arabs are there, they have human rights like everybody else. Is there any truth in the accusations that Amnesty makes of ethnic cleansing, of removing those Arab villagers?*

SMM: Actually, our principles are not like that. We believe in democracy, we believe in dialogue, we believe even that all the issues could be solved with a democracy, with a discussion. That's what we believe. We respect these institutions like Amnesty International, Human Rights Watch and so on. We respect them and their decisions. But the recent reports you have mentioned – it was in abnormal conditions, I mean it was a war in Tal Abyad. And in war conditions, usually the civilians escape the place of the war. At this time you can find some people, and this report depended on some witnesses who were in Turkey, and not in the area. We invited them to come in and see actual villages, especially after the war was finished.

And they didn't come in. Really, we want them to come. I'm not ignoring … we have made some mistakes. There could be some mistakes. But you can help us to remedy these mistakes. I'm not saying everything is perfect, but it is our principle that we can solve everything with dialogue. And if there are any mistakes, they could be repaired. No problem. But this report, I think it was unfair because they depended on some witnesses who were not in the area. And it was wartime. Of course, you can't ask a civilian to stay in the battlefield, because fighting is going on. And it was the same for Kobane, the other areas. The civilians came out until the battle was finished, and then they came back. And now all the people they were talking about are back in their areas. In Manbij they say the same, they claimed the same happened in Manbij, and now you can see in Manbij, all the people are able to do what they want. And now, the problem is they don't allow the journalists to come in. Anybody who wants to investigate, who wants to research the situation about human rights, to ask about the situation, they don't allow them. So if you are sincere about the claims you're making about us, allow the journalists in to write about the reality. Allow the researchers to come in and research what is going on. They don't allow them. They just make claims that they are doing so and so. I think if they like you, you can come any time. But they have to find their way to Rojava, to visit, and make the report as what they can see, especially [gestures to audience] Mr. David Phillips [director, Columbia University, Institute for the Study of Human Rights]. You are invited to come in.

CR: *One of the difficulties which you face internationally is the historic association between you, the YPG, the Kurdistan Workers' Party (PKK), and Abdullah Ocalan, of course. And this has allowed Turkey to utilise ferocious propaganda against you, against the YPG, that you – like the PKK – are what they call 'terrorists'. And the PKK is of course a listed organisation, both in the EU and the United States. What would you say about your situation vis à vis that of the Turkish Kurds today, and indeed the PKK. Very different political situations, but an historic connection that can't be denied.*

SMM: There are some realities on the ground, everybody knows it, which is Mr. Ocalan. Ocalan is the philosopher, the leader not only of the Kurdish people, but of the Middle East because of his ideas, his philosophy. There are many Arab organisations and institutions which are defending Mr. Ocalan's ideas and visions for the future. We are one of them. The PKK is, maybe, partly, one of them. The PKK is a Kurdistani party. We have relations with all the Kurdistani parties, like the Patriotic Union of Kurdistan (PUK), like Gorran, like Islamic parties – you can see many of them here. We have very good relations with everybody. And we have relations with the PKK, also. It doesn't mean we have organic relations. We are our party, the PYD, and the YPG and the others, we are in Rojava, we are taking care of our people in Rojava, and defending them politically, and what is needed we are doing in Rojava and our decision is made in Rojava. So, if we have some sympathy with some parties, some leaders, I think it's related to all the Kurds. And we don't see the PKK as a terrorist organisation – they are defenders, they are defending the rights of people in North Kurdistan. We believe in that. Nobody can harm this sympathy. As you know, especially since we are talking about Rojava, I am from Kobane and we have in Kobane, if you go to the graveyard in Kobane, you see the martyred people over there. You can see they are from Van, from Mahabad, from Sulaymaniyah, from Qamishli – all of them are there, martyrs from all parts. The blood of these martyrs makes the unification between all the Kurds. So, this is what we are trying to keep: just to be honest with our martyrs' blood. This is something different from having organic relations with the PKK. Everybody is just trying to do for the Kurds, defending their democratic rights anywhere. Turkey is trying to terrorise them. And the only way to do it is to connect them with the PKK. Already, they have put the PKK in the terrorist list without maybe the wishes of some parties. They have forced them to do it.

Transcribed by Sam Keely
Video at
http://web.guengl.streamovations.be/index.php/event/stream/the-european-union-turkey-and-the-kurds

A democratic republic?

Hatip Dicle

Mr Dicle, co-chair of the Democratic Society Congress, provided this briefing about Kurds in Turkey to the international conference on the EU, Turkey, the Middle East and the Kurds, which met at the European Parliament, Brussels, 7-8 December 2016.

The Democratic Society Congress [DTK] is a civil society assembly made up of parties, trade unions, foundations, associations, and elected representatives of the people in Kurdistan of Turkey. Apart from the Kurds, representatives of various ethnic and faith groups who live in Kurdistan are represented in our Congress. Its aim is to develop democracy in Kurdistan, to institutionalise it, and make a contribution to a peaceful, democratic solution to the Kurdish question.

From a total of 501 delegates, 60 per cent are popularly elected, while 40 per cent are representatives of civil society organisations and independent persons. Just like parliaments, the Congress has a working system based on commissions. Today it is facing severe repression and obstruction from the Turkish authorities.

The nation state of the Republic of Turkey was established on part of Ottoman territory following the Sykes-Picot agreement [of 1916]. The founding paradigm of this state entailed different ethnicities, first and foremost the Kurdish people, being subjected to denial of their identity, forced assimilation, and a process of eradication in the mangle of a policy of Turkification. The same policy was implemented against Alevi, Yazidi and Christian communities. The Kurdish people rose in revolt against this tyranny in various parts of Kurdistan between 1924 and 1938. These uprisings were brutally suppressed, but this did not alter the reality that the Kurdish question remained at the top of the political agenda in Turkey.

Hence, in 1984, the armed struggle under the leadership of the PKK [Kurdistan

Workers' Party] began under these objective conditions. Former Turkish President Süleyman Demirel called this latest uprising the 29th Kurdish revolt, which is an expression of the depth of this question.

Despite this reality, the Turkish state has still not abandoned its 93-year-old policy regarding the Kurdish question, which is based on denial and violence. It has been unable to change its mentality and search for a democratic solution. It has been unable to evolve from an oligarchic republic into a democratic one.

I plainly stress this truth: the Kurds believe that their problems can be resolved within the borders of the Republic of Turkey, in the framework of political dialogue and through democratic methods. They wish for their national identity to be recognised in the constitution and to benefit from the language, culture, political and other rights safeguarded by international conventions. They also desire a political status that would enable them to attain self-government, as has been realised in many democratic countries, and are waging a struggle for these goals.

In this context, we have for years proposed that an administrative-political system similar to the one that exists in Spain, with 20 to 25 autonomous regions, each with its own local parliament and government, with devolved powers, apart from foreign affairs, national defence, fiscal matters, and the judicial system, be introduced in Turkey. In this system of devolved government all ethnic and faith groups would be able to organise themselves freely. In brief, the Kurds have always been in favour of a peaceful solution to the problem, but the state has not demonstrated the necessary political will to achieve a resolution. I am one of the living witnesses to efforts that have been made by the Kurdish side to find a peaceful solution, having been involved in talks with delegations from the government since 1993 until the most recent talks in 2013-2015.

In 1993, I was an MP for Diyarbakır in the Turkish Parliament for the DEP [Democracy Party], which was closed down. Following appeals from high-ranking state officials and political parties, including the DEP, PKK leader Mr Ocalan declared a one-month unilateral ceasefire on 17 March 1993. This step created great hopes and expectations for a peaceful solution on the Kurdish side and in democratic circles.

The Turkish President at the time, Turgut Özal, sent a group of DEP MPs, including myself, and Mr Jalal Talabani, the leader of the PUK [Patriotic Union of Kurdistan], who later became President of Iraq, to Lebanon to meet Mr Ocalan to suggest he make the ceasefire indefinite. The talks went well and at a press conference which we attended, on 16 April 1993, Mr Ocalan declared that the ceasefire would last indefinitely.

However, on 17 April, before we had left Damascus to return to Turkey, we received the news that President Özal had died. The timing of his death seemed suspicious. Subsequently, political circles and the Özal family claimed that the President had been murdered by a clique within the state that opposed a political resolution to the Kurdish question. The truth of this has never been confirmed, but following his death Turkey was once again dragged into a maelstrom of bloodshed and violence. We Kurdish MPs who were part of the delegation received long prison sentences.

PKK leader Mr Ocalan declared two more unilateral ceasefires in 1995 and 1998. However, just as in 1993, the Turkish state ignored these efforts. After Mr Ocalan was captured and handed over to Turkey on 15 February 1999, in an international conspiracy, the guerrillas withdrew to South Kurdistan (Northern Iraq) for five years. Although not one single bullet was fired during that time, the state did not take advantage of the historic opportunity.

During this period the European Union and the United States should have been encouraging Turkey to seek a peaceful solution to the Kurdish question. Unfortunately, at the beginning of 2002, the PKK was included, first by the US and then by the EU, on their 'lists of terrorist organisations'. This encouraged Turkey to return once again to its belligerent policy *vis-à-vis* the Kurdish question. The Kurds saw this unfortunate decision as a historic injustice that did not serve a peaceful and political solution to the problem.

In our opinion the correct position for the EU to take is that of a recent decision of a Brussels court, that the conflict in Turkey with Kurdish guerrillas is a 'war', that according to the Geneva Convention the PKK should be accepted as a party to conflict, and thus to remove the PKK from its list of terrorist organisations. I believe that such a realistic approach would make a great contribution to a peaceful and political solution and would be an important step on the path of democracy and peace.

Mr Ocalan has been in prison on İmralı Island for nearly 18 years and is accepted as the *de facto* 'main negotiator' by the state, After he made a proposal that was agreed by the AKP [Justice and Development Party] government, talks were carried on from the beginning of 2013 until 5 April 2015. I was a member of the İmralı delegation as the co-chair of the Democratic Society Congress (DTK) for the last 7 months of this period. During this time, I went to Qendîl in South Kurdistan on many occasions in order to inform PKK administrators of the talks going on at the roundtable on İmralı island. Written records of these talks were shared both with the state delegation and with Mr Ocalan.

As a result of all these efforts a road map consisting of ten articles was drawn up, called the ‘Dolmabahçe Accord’, which in our opinion is a historic document. The aim of this road map was to achieve a breakthrough for a democratic republic in Turkey. In accordance with this, representatives of interested parties were to attend talks that would last for several months, reaching agreement on each article, and after the necessary legal and constitutional steps had been agreed it was to be signed by all parties. For instance, representatives of the Alevi community were to put forward their own demands and after agreement had been reached were to add their signatures. Similar talks were to have been held with the Kurds, minorities, women, workers, etc. A ‘Monitoring Council’ consisting of seven or eight persons agreed by the parties was to have witnessed the proceedings and to have helped resolve difficulties. All these discussions at İmralı were to have been published in the media and agreement reached countrywide. Of course, all these documents were to have given direction to the new democratic constitution that was to have been drafted in Turkey. Ultimately, Turkey was to have become a democratic republic.

At the conclusion of these negotiations, Mr Ocalan was to have made an appeal to the PKK to hold a congress that would reach a decision to end the armed struggle that has been continuing since 1984. PKK administrators had even begun preparations for this. However, the expected did not happen, as President Erdoğan knocked over the negotiating table at İmralı on 5 April 2015, ending the process.

President Erdoğan, along with ISIS [Islamic State of Iraq and the Levant], declared war on the Kurdish people all over the Middle East. Towns and cities in Kurdistan were destroyed by tanks and artillery. The HDP [Peoples’ Democratic Party] co-chairs, several Kurdish MPs and elected mayors were arrested, and municipalities run by the DBP [Democratic Regions Party] were handed over to government appointed trustees. Turkey has been transformed into a prison, with journalists, intellectuals and politicians arrested and tens of thousands of public servants sacked. All these fascistic measures are part and parcel of this war.

It is clear that Erdoğan is taking steps to institutionalise a dark dictatorship in Turkey, under the guise of an executive presidential system. He wants to liquidate the last glimmer of democracy and eliminate hopes of peace. Just like Hitler, he is bellowing for war in the country and abroad. If I have to spell it out, I can say: if Erdoğan cannot be stopped, he wants to put an end to peace, not only in Turkey, but also in the Middle East and the whole world.

I wish to say to all those mediating, peace-loving friends who are trying to contribute to a just, lasting and honourable peace for the Kurdish question: in the same way that it is important during negotiations for the guns to fall silent and for ideas to be heard, of equal importance is safeguarding the health and security of Mr Ocalan, and ensuring his complete freedom in the shortest time possible. These steps should be taken decisively in order that the path to peace and democracy is transformed from a dream into reality.

Finally, I would like to say that we in Turkey and in Kurdistan who are in favour of peace and the fraternity of peoples, and everyone who supports democracy, will be together and resist, and we will most certainly win. Our hopes are steadfast and we are resolute and determined.

* * *

There follows a dossier of elected representatives of the People's Democratic Party (HDP) who have been arrested in Turkey in recent months. The dossier is dated 12 January 2017, since when arrests have continued. On Saturday 28 January, when British Prime Minister Theresa May became the first western political leader to visit President Erdogan since the July coup, three more HDP Members of the Turkish Parliament were unlawfully detained. They are Istanbul MP Hüda Kaya, Diyarbakır MP Altan Tan and Adana MP Meral Danış Beştaş. The next day, HDP Spokesperson and Kars MP Ayhan Bilgen was detained. A referendum to extend President Erdogan's considerable powers is scheduled for April 2017. In this context, political repression of the HDP and other groups is likely to intensify.

HDP
HALKLARIN DEMOKRATİK PARTİSİ
PEOPLES' DEMOCRATIC PARTY

THE END OF DEMOCRACY IN TURKEY AND THE NEW DICTATORSHIP

INFORMATION FILE ON ARRESTED MPs OF PEOPLE'S DEMOCRATIC PARTY – HDP

Index:

Summary about the latest situation

HDP co-chair Demirtas brought to prison

On the 3rd of November, the purge of President Erdogan against our party has reached another peak: our Co-Chairs **Selahattin Demirtas** and **Figen Yüksekdag**, along with ten further Members of Parliament (MP) of our party, namely **Nursel Aydogan**, **Idris Baluken**, **Leyla Birlik**, **Ferhat Encü**, **Selma Irmak**, **Sirri Süreyya Önder**, **Ziya Pir**, **Imam Tascier**, **Gülser Yildirim** and **Abdullah Zeydan** have been detained across Turkey. **Demirtas**, **Yüksekdag**, **Aydogan**, **Baluken**, **Birlik**, **Encü**, **Irmak**, **Zeydan**, **Nihat Akdogan** and **Yildirim** have been arrested by court order and sent to prison. **Pir**, **Önder** and **Tascier** have been released on probation. More arrests are to be expected. Within the scope of the operation, police also raided the HDP headquarters in Turkish capital Ankara and attacked the HDP deputies and members inside. Police later blocked all the roads leading to the building with barricades. Even the party members and deputies are not allowed access to the building amid intense measures and mobilization by police forces in large numbers.

The goal of these measures is to shut down the third largest party in parliament. This is a dark day not only for our party but for all of Turkey and the region as it means the end of democracy in Turkey.

Ever since our party reached a **historic victory** during the national elections of June 7, 2015, when we succeeded to enter parliament despite the undemocratic 10% threshold, President Erdogan has singled out our party as the main target of his authoritarian policies. The reason is our principled opposition against his goal to introduce a presidential system in Turkey. Our seats in parliament are the biggest obstacles to the necessary constitutional changes. Thus, he simply ordered new elections in November 2015. Despite a series of violent assaults by "unknown perpetrators" on our party members and infrastructure, we managed once again to surpass the threshold on November 5, 2015 and won 59 seats in Parliament. Since he could not re-order elections another time, President Erdogan initiated the lifting of the immunity of our MPs in May 2016. **As he could not prevent us from entering Parliament, he now orders us into prison.**

DBP co-chair and former MP Sebahat Tuncel arrested with violent force

Thousands of members, executives, elected mayors and city council members affiliated with the HDP and/or our sister party DBP have already been sent to prison on groundless charges since our electoral victory in June 2015. The co-chair and former MP Sebahat Tuncel are amongst the arrested. Yet the coup attempt on July 15, 2016 and the subsequent declaration of a state of emergency has been the welcome opportunity for President Erdogan to eliminate all opposition. **There is no freedom of expression and no freedom of press, no academic freedom, and no fair and independent judicial system any more.** With government decrees gaining the power of law, over 170 media outlets critical of Erdogan have been banned. More than 130 journalists are in prison, including world-renowned authors and intellectuals. Most recently, two Kurdish news agencies and several Kurdish dailies were closed down and the chief-editor, columnists and journalists of the daily Cumhuriyet have been detained. More than 80,000 people have been detained since July 15, and about half of them are in prison now.

Co-mayors of Diyarbakir Mr. Firat Anli and former MP Ms. Gulten Kisanak

On October 30, Ms. **Gülten Kisanak** and Mr. **Firat Anli**, elected co-mayors of Diyarbakir from our party, were arrested and sent to prison. A district governor from Ankara was appointed to run the municipality. With this, the number of Kurdish municipalities run by bureaucrats appointed by the central government increased to 28. **About 30 democratically elected Kurdish mayors are now in prison, and about 70 of them were dismissed by the central government.**

We strongly condemn the arrests of our Co-Chairs Selahattin Demirtas, Figen Yüksekdag as well as our MPs and demand their immediate release. The manufactured charges against them and all other party members must be dropped. **History has shown over and over again that any power based on brute force is outlived by the struggle for justice and freedom.** We will not surrender to these dictatorial policies and call upon our friends around the world to stand in solidarity in our struggle to prevent Erdogan to steer the country into a civil war and further despotism.

Joint Defense Statement of Peoples' Democratic Party (HDP) MPs

The Peoples' Democratic Party (HDP) that I represent received over six million votes in 7 June 2015 general elections, passing the 10% election threshold and winning 80 seats in the Parliament. Our democratic ballot box victory ended the single-party rule of Justice and Development Party (AKP), and prevented it from drafting a new Constitution on its own. President Recep Tayyip Erdoğan, who aims to establish his "one-man rule" in the country and who have not hesitated to resort to all kinds of illegalities to fulfil this aim, did not respect this election result. He prevented the formation of any coalition government and called for a snap election. Meanwhile, Mr Erdoğan also ended the almost three-year-long peace process (with the Kurdish movement), having seen it not fitting to serve his interests and to enlarge his electoral base, and dragged the country into an enflamed conflict process.

This conflict environment created among our citizen's due concerns about security. Amidst this climate of shock and fear, snap elections were held under conditions that were far from being fair and free. The AKP won the elections on 1 November 2015 and formed a single-party government again.

After hearing the June 7 election results, Mr Erdoğan staged in great panic and haste a political coup in the country by superseding the Parliament and the Government, by taking the judiciary under control to a great extent and by monopolizing the media. He went so far as to publicly announce having seized the state by declaring himself not being bound by the Constitution, by declaring the *de facto* change of the regime, and by declaring that he did not recognize the decisions of the Constitutional Court.

Mr Erdoğan himself faces serious allegations of being involved in numerous criminal activities while holding the Office of the Prime Ministry, including bribery, theft, money laundering, conducting the gold trade with Iran in contravention of international embargo, and supplying terrorist operatives in Syria with arms. He has so far been successful in obstructing investigation of these allegations with the pressure and control that he established over the judiciary.

Mr Erdoğan is aware that the only way to effectively cover-up his crimes is to monopolize all powers in his hands. It is evident that he will not refrain from doing anything short of crazy to this end. He has soaked the country in blood, and has succeeded in inflaming nationalist and chauvinist feelings and racial hate discourse in public by sending coffins to all four corners of the country. Mr Erdoğan is getting closer to his personal goals step by step with the support of popular masses whom he had lured into loyalty to serve him with the lie, "the homeland is under the threat of partition."

HDP is the only obstacle before Mr Erdoğan to attain his goal; that is, to establish a dictatorship under the guise of a presidential system. Our party's passing the election threshold for a second time in the general elections of 1 November and entering the parliament by winning 59 seats prevented Mr Erdoğan from gaining the majority necessary to change the Constitution relying on the AKP legislators alone. That is why he has been endeavoring for another possible snap or interim election that might secure parliamentary majority composed of at least 367 AKP MPs loyal to him. [1]

Our party HDP brings together representatives of all different etno-linguistic and religious groups that make up Turkey's multicultural, multilingual, multi-religious societal fabric. We represent Turks, Kurds, Arabs, Armenians, Turkmen, Assyrians, Ezidis, and many other ethnic groups, who believe that it is possible to live together in equality and justice. We believe that the only way to sustain this co-existence is a pluralist democracy backed by strong local democracy and autonomy.

Our party HDP fully embraces women's struggle for freedom and liberty. Guaranteeing women`s equal participation in politics, our party has so far achieved the highest representation of female MPs in Turkey's parliamentary politics. The lifting of immunities of all of our party`s female MPs is a threat for all women in Turkey and an assault on their struggle.

We oppose all forms of violence and believe in the power of dialogue and negotiation in solving all problems. Mr Erdoğan, who aims to consolidate a fascist rule of one man, one language, and one sect, perceives this stance of the HDP also as an ideological "threat."

It is for these reasons that Mr Erdoğan has targeted the HDP ever since it entered politics. After repeatedly failing to prevent our party's electoral success despite all sorts of tricks, injustices, attacks, and bombings, Mr Erdoğan forced the lifting our parliamentary immunities by sidestepping the constitution and the parliamentary bylaws. As someone whose own independence and impartiality are heavily debated in public, he is now trying to persecute us in so-called trials.

The AKP Government that lifted our immunities has bestowed an immunity shield upon the military without losing any time, in an attempt to elude imminent judicial processes concerning the crimes committed by the army in Kurdish cities especially during the last one year. The Army that was provided with the immunity shield on 14 July 2016 made a Coup Attempt on 15 July 2016. Since the 7th of June 2015, the AKP Government with its push for a policy of conflict escalation and its exclusion of democratic politics by putting in effect policies of war since has strengthened the hand of the coupists who went so wild as to bombard the Parliament. Even though the failed coup attempt presented an opportunity to achieve over-arching social peace through a settlement on the basis of democratic principles, Erdoğan and the AKP Government decided to move into a state of emergency regime and began to govern the whole country through Decrees with Power of Law issued by the Cabinet. Whereas it was necessary to utilize this failed coup attempt in favor of democracy, it was used to move into the process of another coup. Appointment of trustees to elected municipalities and the suspension of thousands of teachers are the most concrete indicators of the construction of a new coup regime by means of these Decrees with Power of Law. Erdoğan and AKP whose war policies put into action before 7 June elections laid the groundwork for a coup, have created the conditions for the process that led all the way to the 15 July coup attempt. The policies that have been implemented after 15 July and the anti-democratic concept which appears to have been put into action keep consolidating the grounds for a civil war. Even though the only way out of this chaos is to strengthen democratic politics and put

[1] A parliamentary majority of 367 votes is needed to make any amendments in the Constitution.

an end to military/civilian regimes of political tutelage, practices that will take the country back tens of years in time show us painfully that this is not the path chosen.

We are the elected representatives of people. We do not represent ourselves, but the people who elected us. Right now, I am standing before you as a member of the parliament entitled to legislative immunity. I cannot allow disrespect be done to the electoral will of my people and this identity that I represent.

I have no qualms about accounting for my deeds before a fair and impartial tribunal. I did nothing that I cannot account for. Yet I shall never accept being the subject of a political prosecution which seeks to stand at attention before Power at this time when the credibility of the judiciary in our country has sunk to the bottom. I carry no suspicion and disrespect for you as a person. Yet I refuse to be a puppet in this mocked prosecution which takes place only because Erdoğan, who himself has a heavily blotted political history, has ordered it.

I shall not answer any questions that you would ask me. I do not believe that you will conduct a fair trial by any means. It is already against the law that I am brought to here. A politician's counterparts in the political arena are other politicians, and not members of the judiciary. As members of the judiciary, you yourselves should refuse to be a party in political games or plots. You are bound with universal and democratic principles of law as well as the international conventions that Turkey has signed and integrated into its Constitution.

We shall resolutely continue our political struggle until a pluralist democratic regime is established and peace and serenity is achieved in our country. We shall continue defending living together in equality against societal polarization and antagonism. We shall continue defending democratic political struggle against violence. We shall continue standing against monism by advocating pluralism, and against fascism by advocating democracy. We shall continue opposing sectarian and racist politics by defending freedom of religion and conscience. We shall continue opposing discrimination and hate speech by advocating equality. And of course we shall continue in our defense of equality and of all the rights that Kurdish people are entitled to because they are a people. We shall continue advocating for the Alevi community's demand for equal citizenship rights, and for freedom of belief for all religious minorities. We shall continue our struggle for women's equal participation in social, political and economic life. We shall continue our struggle to protect the environment and ecology against capitalist destruction. We shall continue defending labor from the greed of capital for more profits, and advocating for workers' rights. Irrespective of whether we are in prison or in parliament, you will not be able to prevent us from struggling for these ideals.

We have no doubt that we will get rid of this fascist order that has been imposed on us and on our country for the sake of a presidential system. Sooner or later, our democratic struggle will prevail. This dilapidated regime of Mr Erdoğan is but going to change.

I have no demand or expectation from you. ***It is only my people who have elected me can question my political activities.***

Profiles and Messages from the Arrested MP's

Selahattin Demirtaş:

Co-Chair and MP representing Istanbul. Mr. Demirtaş was born in Diyarbakır, Turkey in 1973. He enrolled at Ankara University Law Faculty. After college, Demirtaş worked as a freelance lawyer for a time before becoming a member of the executive committee of the Diyarbakır Branch of the Human Rights Association (IHD). During his term as chair, the association focused heavily on the increasing unsolved political murders in Turkey. Demirtaş is among the founding members of the Turkish Human Rights Association (TIHV) and the Diyarbakır post of Amnesty International. He has 93 lawsuits issued by the prosecutors from 18 different provinces. In total, 486 years of imprisonment and two aggravated life imprisonments are indicted by the prosecutors.

Mr. Demirtas' message: Firstly, greetings and love to all friends. In these days where our country is pushed further into darkness, our illegal arrest only served to intensify the darkness. However, those that think that they can make us surrender to this darkness should remember that one piece of match or one candle is enough to lighten up this darkness. Whatever our location or conditions may be, we will continue to burn like a candle so that our people can live in peace in free days to come. Everyone should be part of the struggle for democracy and work towards our bright future. My morale and health are good. With love.

Figen Yüksekdağ:

Co-Chair of the HDP and MP representing Van. Ms. Yüksekdağ was born 1971 in Gölovası, Yumurtalık, Adana Province, into an ethnically Turkish farming family. She is the current coleader of the Peoples' Democratic Party (HDP) of Turkey as of 2014, serving alongside Selahattin Demirtaş. She was an independent parliamentary candidate for the Adana electoral district in the 2002 general election. She was involved in women's rights movements for several years before becoming the editor of the Socialist Woman magazine. While serving on the board of the Atılım newspaper, she was taken into custody in 2009 due to her political activity. She cofounded the Socialist Party of the Oppressed (ESP) shortly after in 2010 and resigned as leader in 2014 to join the HDP. She has 21 lawsuits against her.

Ms. Yüksekdağ's message: Despite everything, they cannot end our hopes and break our resistance. HDP is the only hope for freedom and democracy in Turkey, whether we are inside or outside prison. This is why they are scared. Nobody should be demoralized or put down their guard. Nobody should forget that this hatred and hostility is out of fear. Love and courage will win. With love and greetings.

İdris Baluken:

MP representing Diyarbakır. Mr. Baluken, born in 1976 in Bingöl, currently serves as a parliamentary group leader of the HDP since April 2014. He previously served as a parliamentary group leader for the Peace and Democracy Party (BDP) from 2012. He graduated from Ankara University Faculty of Medicine. He worked as a doctor in Bingöl and Diyarbakır for many years. He has been involved in the administration of the Turkish Thoracic Society, the Turkish Medical Association and the Health and Social Service Workers Union Diyarbakır branch. He is married with two children. Joined several national and international academic studies. Married with two children. He has 23 lawsuits.

Mr. Baluken's message: Our people should keep their morale high, I salute our people that stand up for their honor. We are standing up for our honor too. Those that are supposed to be here are not us but those that have prepared this conspiracy. They are hiding where we are in order to marginalize us. This is the policy of kidnapping and taking hostages. Throughout history, this mentality has always been defeated. We will continue to preserve our stance and continue our struggle wherever we are. Greetings to our people.

Leyla Birlik:

MP representing Şırnak Province Born in Mardin/Derik in 1974. She was the chair of the City Council of Şırnak Province. She continues her oil painting works. Fluent in Kurdish and Turkish. Married with one child. She has 8 lawsuits.

Ms. Birlik's message:

We will resist here, in prison, and outside. And we will certainly prevail. Greetings.

Ferhat Encü:

MP representing Şırnak Province. Born in Şırnak/Uludere in 1985. Studied Mining Engineering at Çukurova University, Adana. He lost 34 relatives during the bombardment of Turkish air forces at Roboski Village on 28 December 2011. Fluent in Kurdish and Turkish. He has 17 lawsuits.

Mr. Encü's message: This is a struggle, and thousands have fallen for this struggle. We are no different from them. This is a violent wave of attacks, but can be repelled with resistance. We are resisting here, and we will continue. Nobody should be unhappy, the honorable resistance of those that keep their hopes alive will prevail. Hope is also uniting, the honorable resistance of our people against fascism will prevail. Nobody can call themselves free in a country where our Co-Presidents are taken hostage. I send my greetings and love to our people.

Gülser Yıldırım:

MP representing Mardin Province. Born in 1963 in Mardin/Nusaybin. She became active in politics in 2000 as a member of the Women Branch of the HADEP (People's Democracy Party). She was an executive member of Free Party, DEHAP, DTP and BDP. She was imprisoned in 2010 for four years due to her political activities. Fluent in Kurdish and Turkish. Married, mother of 4 children. She has 11 lawsuits.

Ms. Yıldırım's message: No matter what the AKP dictatorship does, we will never give up from our struggle and the values were believe in. AKP's inhumane policies show how right the struggle we have been waging against the AKP has been. I want our people to know that we are more determined. Greetings and love.

Nursel Aydoğan:

MP representing Diyarbakir. Born in 1958 in Bursa/Yenisehir. Studied Food Engineering at Hacettepe University in Ankara and then worked as Food Engineer for several years. She was the executive member of trade union SES before her election to the Parliament in 2011. She has 44 lawsuits.

Ms. Aydoğan's message: Our arrests are part of the elimination of the HDP. They should not forget that the HDP is a party with a cause. Even if we are in prison, we will follow our cause and struggle. Nobody's morale should be affected by our arrests; nobody should ever lose hope. No matter what the AKP decides to do, we will keep our morale high. We will grow our hope

Selma Irmak:

MP representing Hakkari. Born in 1971 in Mardin/Kızıltepe and moved to Konya in 1978. She attended Konya Selçuk University for preschool teacher education but arrested for political reasons. She was imprisoned for 3 years and 9 months. She became an active member of the Democratic People Party (DEHAP) after she was released. She then became the executive board member of the Mesopotamian Cultural Centre and the Kurdish Institute of Istanbul. She returned back to Konya and elected as the chairperson for the Konya Branch of the DEHAP. She participated in the formation of the Democratic Society Party (DTP) and elected as general accountant of the DTP. She was elected to the parliament from Şırnak in 2011 and was a member of the foreign affairs commission of the Parliament. She was reelected to the Parliament from Hakkari both in the 7 June and 1 November 2015 elections. Fluent in Kurdish and Turkish. She has 22 lawsuits.

Ms. Irmak's message: AKP's coup has become apparent. This coup targets the democracy front and is sneakier than the 1980 coup. It is based on the fear of widespread opposition. Resistance will continue as our people resist out there and we resist in here. Prisons are our second homes. My special greetings to woman comrades. Women will be the AKP's nightmare. Our people should stand up for their future. We call upon the people of Turkey and Kurdistan to resist. Greetings and love.

Nihat Akdogan:

MP epresenting Hakkari Province Born in 1980 in Hakkari. Studied Public Relations at Anadolu University. He was a member of the Party Assembly of the HDP before his election to the Parliament on 7 June 2015. He has 8 lawsuits.

Mr. Akdogan's Message: The democracy will win and the end

TURKEY: The country where democracy, human rights, freedom and the rule of law has come to an end and replaced with battlefields, destruction and dungeons.

The Turkish Governments enmity of democracy and Kurds continues

BALANCE-SHEET FOR ATTACKS ON ELECTED REPRESENTATIVES AND MUNICIPALITIES

The AKP's attacks continue at full speed. Alongside Peoples Democratic Party (HDP) co-chairs, MP's and Democratic Regions Party (DBP) co-chair, the AKP-Erdogan have taken hostage, the co-chairs of 50 DBP municipalities and seized the will of 43 DBP councils.

The AKP-Erdogan regime has failed to implement what they want in Kurdistan until now, turning the 'state of emergency' into an opportunity, the attacks against the gains of the Kurdish people continue uninterrupted. In the 7 June 2015 elections, the AKP regime failed in Kurdistan, unable to get any MP's elected in the region. This triggered the start of the AKP regimes war concept against the Kurdish people, through the isolation policy on the Kurdish leader Abdullah Ocalan.

The concept of denial and annihilation launched against Kurdish towns by AKP gangs was countered by the self-defence of Kurdish youth on the basis of resistance for self-administration. The AKP-Erdogan, with no compliance to rules of war, not only burnt and destroyed Kurdish towns but brought the towns ***Cizre, Sur, Nusaybin, Idil, Gever, Silvan*** and ***Sirnak*** to the ground with tanks and bombs. ***Only in Cizre, 103 civilians were burnt alive. Hundreds of people were massacred. 1.5 million people were forced to migrate during and after these massacres***. The AKP regime then went on to implement its genocidal attacks against the Municipalities and councils of these towns, which are the gains of the Kurdish people.

46 CO-CHAIRS HAVE BEEN DISMISSED, 50 ARRESTED

The attacks against Kurdish politics and political representatives continue. In this context, the arrests include, amongst the HDP MP's, co-chairs ***Selahattin Demirtas*** and ***Figen Yuksekdag***, DBP co-chair ***Sebahat Tuncel***, Free Women's Congress (KJA) spokesperson ***Ayla Akat Ata***, and Amed Municipality co-chairs ***Gulten Kisanak*** and ***Firat Anli***. Also, many more municipality and council co-chairs, Central Executive Board (MYK) and Party Council (PM) and party members have been arrested. Turkey has almost been turned into an open prison camp, with the immeasurable unlawful activity committed by the government. The denial and annihilation policies brought to life by the AKP in the Kurdish cities, towns and neighbourhoods are due to the popularity of Kurdish politics and the Kurdish struggle, represented by the latest elections.

There have been government trustees appointed, officially to 34 DBP held municipalities and de facto appointments to 4 DBP municipalities till date. In total, there has been a civil-coup against 50 DBP held municipalities. Turkey's deepening chaos lead by the AKP/Palace is exemplified by the dismissal of 46 DBP co-chairs, the arrests of 50 municipality co-chairs, search warrants for 7 DBP municipality co-chairs. Also, 43 DBP municipality co-chairs were released after being arrested or detained, within to the scope of the case.

MUNICIPALITIES WITH APPOINTED TRUSTEES AND THEIR VOTING RATES

Van, Mardin Metropolitan municipalities, along with ***Dersim*** and ***Siirt*** municipalities and the 4 de facto municipalities, alongside ***Amed*** Metropolitan municipality make up the 43 municipalities seized by the government by appointed trustees.

The voting rates for some seized DBP municipalities in the last elections:

1. DBP votes, 55.89% for Batman municipality. Appointed Government trustee, Şeref Aksoy.
2. DBP votes, 66.83% for Hakkari municipality. Appointed Government trustee, assistant governor Coney Epçim.
3. DBP votes 48.43% for Diyadin municipality. Appointed Government trustee, district governor Mekan Çeviren.
4. DBP votes, 50.45% for Beşiri municipality. Appointed Government trustee, district governor Mustafa Maslak.
5. DBP votes, 52.43% for Gercüş municipality. Appointed Government trustee, district governor Ünal Koç.
6. DBP votes, 69.55% for Silvan municipality. Appointed Government trustee, district governor Murat Kütük.
7. DBP votes, 54.41% for Sur municipality. Appointed Government trustee, assistant governor Bilal Özkan.
8. DBP votes, 39.08% for Hınıs municipality. Appointed Government trustee, district governor Bülent Ay.
9. DBP votes, 51.67% for Tuzluca municipality. Appointed Government trustee, district governor İbrahim Civelek.
10. DBP votes, 60.16% for Dargeçit municipality. Appointed Government trustee, district governor M. Yaşar Yeşiltaş.
11. DBP votes, 64.4% for Derik municipality. Appointed Government trustee, district governor M. Fatih Saltürk.
12. DBP votes, 61.71% for Mazıdağ municipality. Appointed Government trustee, district governor Halit Benek.
13. DBP votes, 78.78% for Nusaybin municipality. Appointed Government trustee, district governor Ergün Baysal.
14. DBP votes, 45.84% for Bulanık municipality. Appointed Government trustee, district governor Ömer Şahin.
15. DBP votes, 52.37% for Eruh municipality. Appointed Government trustee, district governor Murat Dayanç.
16. DBP votes, 52.58% for Suruç municipality. Appointed Government trustee, district governor Tarık Açıkgöz
17. DBP votes, 81.61% for Cizre municipality. Appointed Government trustee, district governorAhmet Adanur
18. DBP votes, 78.19% for Silopi municipality. Appointed Government trustee, district governor Savaş Konak.
19. DBP votes, 78.9% for İdil municipality. Appointed Government trustee, district governor Ersin Tepeli.
20. DBP votes, 50.91% for Edremit municipality. Appointed Government trustee, district governor İbrahim Özkan.

21. DBP votes, 49.43% for Erciş municipality. Appointed Government trustee, district governor M. Şirin Yaşar.
22. DBP votes, 48.32% for İpekyolu municipality. Appointed Government trustee, Assistant governor Önder Can.
23. DBP votes, 71.62% for Özalp municipality. Appointed Government trustee, district governor Serdar Karal.
24. DBP votes, 56.22% for İkiköpru municipality. Appointed Government trustee, district governor Mustafa Maslak.
25. DBP votes, 61.75% for Hoşhaber municipality. Appointed Government trustee, Assistant governor Bilgehan Karafil.
26. DBP votes, 45.8% for Hani municipality. Appointed Government trustee, district governor Yusuf Turan.
27. DBP votes, 55.32% for Amed Metroplitan municipality. Appointed Government trustee, District governor Cumali Atilla.
28. DBP votes, 60.91% for Şırnak municipality. Appointed Government trustee, Assistant governor Turan Bedirhanoğlu.
29. DBP votes, 63.40% for Varto municipality. Appointed Government trustee, district governor Mehmet Nuri Çetin.
30. DBP votes, 35.12% for Bitlis Ahlat - Ovakışla Municipality.

This clearly shows that the AKP-Palace regime has hijacked the will of the people by, most recently, the seizure of the Siirt municipality, ***Mardin*** Metropolitan municipality, ***Van*** Metropolitan municipality and Dersim municipality, through appointing trustees, totalling a number of 43 DBP held municipalities being officially seized by the government and ***Viransehir, Halfeti*** and ***Bozova*** municipalities being de facto seized by appointing district governors to take over administration.

ARRESTED DBP MUNICIPALITY CO-CHAIRS

1. Adile Kozay - Gever Municipality Deputy Co-Chair
2. Dilek Hatipoğlu - Hakkari Municipality Co-Chair
3. Nurullah Çiftçi - Hakkari Municipality Co-Chair
4. Sevil Rojbin Çetin - Edremit Municipality Co-Chair
5. Handan Bağcı - Van Özalp Municipality Co-Chair
6. Ali Çam - Iğdır Hoşhaber Municipality Co-Chair
7. Diba Keskin - Erçiş Municipality Co-Chair
8. Rahmi Çelik - Bulanık Municipality Co-Chair
9. Burhan Kocaman - Elazığ Karakoçan Municipality Co-Chair
10. Cennet Ayık - Elazığ Karakoçan Municipality Co-Chair
11. Zeynep Şimşik - Dargeçit Municipality Co-Chair
12. Seyran Argan - Beytüşşebap Municipality Co-Chair
13. Abdurrahman Çağan - Erçiş Municipality Co-Chair
14. Abdulkerim Erdem - Derik Municipality Co-Chair
15. Sabahat Çetinkaya - Derik Municipality Co-Chair
16. Hazal Aras - Diyadin Municipality Co-Chair
17. Kasım Ağgün - Iğdır Hoşhaber Municipality Co-Chair
18. Aygün Taşkın - Ergani Municipality Co-Chair
19. Figen Yaşar - Bulanık Municipality Co-Chair
20. Nazmi Çoşkun - Hakkari Municipality Deputy Co-Chair
21. Şerafettin Özalp - Özalp Municipality Co-Chair
22. Nevin Oyman - İdil Municipality Co-Chair
23. Tülay Karaca - Erzurum Tekman Municipality Co-Chair
24. Abdurahman Zorlu - Hani Municipality Co-Chair
25. Mehmet Muhdi Aslan - İdil Municipality Co-Chair
26. Zilan Aldatmaz - Van Saray Municipality Co-Chair
27. Gültan Kışanak - Amed Metroplitan Municipality Co-Chair

28. Fırat Anlı - Amed Metropolitan Municipality Co-Chair
29. Suna Atabay - Van Çaldıran Municipality Co-Chair
30. Ahmet Demir - Ovakışla Municipality Co-Chair
31. Servin Karakoç - Ovakışla Municipality Co-Chair
32. Sabite Ekinci - Varto Municipality Co-Chair
33. Hüseyin Güneş - Varto Municipality Co-Chai
34. Kadir Konur - Cizre Municipality Co-Chair
35. Tuncer Bakırhan - Siirt Municipality Co-Chair
36. Mehmet Ali Bul - Dersim Municipality Co-Chair
37. Nurhayat Altun - Dersim Municipality Co-Chair
38. Rabia Takas - Başverimli (Silopi) Municipality Co-Chair
39. Tahir Aytış - Başverimli (Silopi) Municipality Co-Chair
40. Ahmet Türk - Mardin Municipality Co-Chair
41. Nevin Daşdemir - Bitlis Municipality Co-Chair
42. Hüseyin Olan - Bitlis Municipality Co-Chair
43. Senayet Ata - Güroymak Municipality Co-Chair
44. Mehmet Emin Avras - Güroymak Municipality Co-Chair
45. Halis Coşkun - Malazgirt Municipality Co-Chair
46. Memnune Söylemez - Malazgirt Municipality Co-Chair

Turkish State's Cross Border Attacks into Rojava Go Up Seven-fold in One Year

Since the beginning of the Rojava Revolution, the Turkish state has waged a war against Rojava through several proxies and now its attacks on the border are intensifying.

When the Rojava Revolution started on 19 July, 2012, certain gangs began to openly attack Rojava. The AKP collaborated at the highest level with organisations such as Ahral Al-Sham, Al-nusra and ISIS, in trying to suffocate the Rojava Revolution.

The Rojava Democratic Autonomous Administration has control of almost the entire 911-kilometre-long Turkey-Rojava border; only Jarablus and Rai fall outside its control. The Turkish state, discomforted by this development, is attacking the YPG from Shehba, which it is currently occupying.

The attack against Serekaniye was the first attack

The relationship between the AKP and the terrorist gangs first showed itself on 8 November, 2012, when they attacked Serekaniye. On this day, hundreds of gang members belonging to the FSA were sent into Serekaniye from the Turkish border in an attempt to overrun the city. Concurrently, the Syrian bombed the town with heavy artillery. Many gang members were killed as a result of the YPG's resistance. In one week, 10 civilians were killed, about 70 were injured, 50 houses were destroyed and more than 11 thousand people were left displaced. Many documents seized in the clashes proved the relationship between the gangs and the AKP.

The attack against Kobane was from the same place

Many documents that showed the relationship between the Turkish state and ISIS were captured when ISIS began its attack against Kobani on 13 September, 2014. Information was leaked on how ISIS was using the Turkish border for reinforcements and logistical support and even photos of ISIS fighters posing with Turkish soldiers surfaced at the time.

The Turkish state could not accept the fact that ISIS was defeated in Kobani by the resistance of the YPG and thus played a significant role in the Kobani massacre on 25 June, 2015. In the attack, where the Turkish state allowed for fighters and bomb-laden vehicles to enter the city through its border, a total of 251 civilians were killed, of which 35 were children and 64 were women, and 267 were left injured.

Efforts continuing in Gire Spi

On 27 February of this year, ISIS conducted an attack against Gire Spi, Siluk and Mebruka in the hope of separating the cantons of Kobani and Cizire from each other. In this attack, 23 civilians and 43 YPG/YPJ fighters lost their lives while defending the towns. A total of 291 ISIS fighters were killed during the clashes and 6 were taken captive.

Four days prior to the attack against Gire Spi, the Turkish army carried out artillery attacks against YPG positions from across the border. The Turkish army also continued its artillery support on the day of the attack by ISIS. One YPG fighter was killed in the artillery attacks by the Turkish army and others were injured.

'Both military and civilian positions targeted'

The Turkish state is both logistically supporting the gangs attacking Rojava and is also breaking international rules of engagement by bombarding YPG positions and civilian settlements from across the border.

The Turkish state animosity against the Kurds and Rojava is breaking all international laws. The Turkish state is attacking the civilians working on the fields along the border. In some places, the people are not even allowed to work the fields that are more than a kilometre from the border. The people are being shot at. They are even using thermal cameras to make sure that they do not miss.

22 in 2015, 152 in 2015

They massacred, built walls, dug trenches and cut trees…

In regular statements released by the press centre of the YPG, it was stated that the Turkish army attacked YPG positions from across the border on 22 different occasions. On 4 May, 2015, the Turkish army indiscriminately shot at people in the Raco town of Efrin. The houses of the villagers were damaged and the people were unable to go to their fields.

152 times in the first 10 months of 2016…

In 2016, the attacks of the Turkish army intensified against Rojava. The Turkish state attacked YPG positions and civilian settlement areas on many occasions throughout 2016.

- The Turkish state attacked YPG positions and civilian settlements on 152 occasions (Once in January, 9 times in February, 6 times in March, 14 times in April, 13 times in May, 17 times in June, 22 times in July, 17 times in August, 26 times in September, 17 times in October).
- In these attacks 2 civilians in February, 4 civilians in April, 2 civilians in May in Kobani, I child in June in Gire Spi, 4 civilians and 2 YPG fighters in August, 9 civilians in September and 2 civilians in October were killed.
- In these attacks 1 civilian in February, 4 civilians in April, 2 civilians in May in Kobani, 9 civilians in Gire Spi, 50 civilians and 2 YPG fighters in August, 61 civilians in September and 2 civilians in October were injured.

Air space violated

The AKP-led Turkish state did not just logistically support the gangs and shoot at civilians and YPG fighters. The AKP violated the airspace of the Rojava Democratic Autonomous Region's airspace on numerous occasions with its drones, helicopters and soldiers.

- Throughout the Rojava Revolution the AKP has dug trenches and built walls within the borders of Rojava from the Endiwer village of Derik all the way to Efrin, cutting down trees and occupying the land of the people of Rojava.
- In an action organised by journalists from Rojava against the massacre in Nusaybin, Turkish soldiers were photographed and recorded violating the border on numerous occasions; these were released to the public.
- In the month of August, Turkish soldiers violated the border of Rojava on two occasions using military grade vehicles.
- On two other occasions, helicopters belonging to the Turkish army violated the border.
- An air bombardment was conducted in the canton of Efrin.
- In the month of September, Turkish soldiers crossed into the border of Rojava on 2 occasions and on 3 occasions, drones belonging to the Turkish army entered into Rojava airspace.

The operation is against Raqqa, however…

While making every effort to ensure that the YPG would not be a part of the operation to liberate Raqqa, the AKP's attacks against Rojava in the 17 days since the start of the operation are as follows:

- On the 5th of November at 21:00, a drone was flown over the village of Tilseriye to the west of Kobani and at the same time YPG positions were fired at from the Turkish side of the border.
- On the 6th of November, YPG positions in the village of Ziraveke to the west of Kobane were fired at using heavy artillery from across the border.
- On the 7th of November, the Turkish army tried to take some gang members across the border into Rojava. At about 19:00 a group of 12 gang members were smuggled across in military grade vehicles belonging to the Turkish army into the village of Doda between Qamislo and Amude. While smuggling in the gang members, YPG positions were fired at from the Turkish military vehicle. The gang members retreated back to Turkey after facing fierce resistance from the YPG; two gang members were injured in the clashes. The second location where a group of gang members attempted to enter Rojava was to the west of Kobani. At 19:00 the gang members fell into an YPG controlled area and had to quickly retreat back into Turkey after heavy clashes broke out.
- On the 7th of November, the Turkish army attacked the villages of Gelbenav, Koran and Elsen of Gire Spi.
- On the 8th of November, the Turkish army attacked YPG positions in the villages of Dola Kel Heseneke and Cil Axa of Tirbespiye. The YPG retaliated to these attacks.
- On the 10th, 12th and 13th of November at 18:15, artillery was fired from a Turkish border military station into Cisir Hesarke region of the town of Raco. In the attacks on the 10th of November, one child and one member of the HPC-Jin were killed.
- On the 17th of November, 2 helicopters belonging to the Turkish army flew over the village of Merwaniye in the canton of Efrin.
- In the last week, the Turkish army has begun digging trenches in the villages of Eyn Dîwarê, Kerdîmih, Hav Metre and Habil Hewa and, by doing so, has ruined a huge section of arable land. As a result of the trenches dug by the Turkish army along the River Tigris near the village of Eyn Diware, thousands of hectares of arable land is in danger of being flooded.

EU Turkey Civic Commission

13th INTERNATIONAL CONFERENCE ON
'THE EU, TURKEY, THE MIDDLE EAST AND THE KURDS'

Wednesday 7 & Thursday 8 of December 2016
European Parliament, Brussels

Turkey, the Kurds and the war in the Middle East
Turkey – Democracy suspended
ISIS and the crisis in the Middle East

The final resolution on the 13th Annual EUTCC conference: Kurdish recomendations and demands

Kurdish demands and the denial policy

The Kurds believe that their problems can be resolved within the borders of Turkey through dialogue and democratic methods. They wish their national identity to be recognised in the constitution, and to benefit from cultural and political rights safeguarded by international conventions. They also desire a political status through which to attain self-government, as realised in many democratic countries. Failing to accommodate their demands, the Turkish state has not yet abandoned its 93-year-old policy of denial and violence, proving unable to change its mentality.

- The conference calls upon Turkey to give up the denial and violence policy and to give the Kurds and all the other ethnic and religious groups a guarantee of recognition.

European blackist

After the Kurdish Leader Mr Abdullah Öcalan was abducted and handed over to Turkey on 15 February 1999, guerrilla units withdrew to South Kurdistan (Northern Iraq) where they remained for five years. Even though they did not fire a single bullet, the Turkish state failed to take advantage of this historic opportunity. While the EU and the US should have been encouraging Turkey to seek a peaceful solution, at the beginning of 2002, they blacklisted the PKK. This encouraged Turkey to return once again to its belligerent approach *vis-à-vis* the Kurdish question. The Kurds saw this unfortunate decision as a historic injustice that did not help find a peaceful and political solution to their problem.

The Brussels Court's (41st Kamer [Correctional Raadkamer] on 3 November 2016) recent verdict to the effect that the war in Turkey '… is an armed conflict in the sense of the international humanitarian law' according to the Geneva conventions and Rome Statute

Therefore:

- The PKK should be accepted as a party to the conflict. This reflects the reality about the PKK and
- The PKK should be removed from the 'list of terrorist organisations'. This would make a great contribution to peace, opening the way for a political settlement.

Peace process

Mr Abdullah Öcalan, who has been jailed for nearly 18 years but accepted by the state as the 'main negotiator', made a proposal that was agreed by the AKP government. Talks were carried on from 2013 until 5 April 2015, resulting in a road map consisting of ten articles. Its aim was a breakthrough for a democratic republic in Turkey. Even though PKK administrators began preparing for this, on 5 April 2015 Erdogan derailed the process. Therefore, the EUTCC conference:

- Calls for the support of the 'Freedom for Öcalan Campaign' launched by the major British trade unions the GMB and UNITE in April 2016, who called for the release of Mr Öcalan as an essential element for a peace process to be successful.
- Calls for restarting the peace process, freeing Mr Öcalan so that he has the freedom to create his negotiation team, and free contact and movement.

Mr Abdullah Öcalan under constant threat

Our conference received the information that AKP-MHP circles are discussing the elimination of Mr Abdullah Öcalan. In fact, those discussing this are asking different parties what the results of this action could be. Commentators have also said that the reintroduction of capital punishment being brought onto the agenda to shape public opinion is also within this framework. We do not know how true these claims are. However, we are receiving information that this is being done to prepare the groundwork for Mr Öcalan's elimination. Any attack on Mr Öcalan will affect not only Kurds and Turkey but will also have an impact on whole world.

- For this reason and urgency, we are calling for immediate sensitivity to this threat from primarily the Kurdish people, the EU, relevant international organisations and public opinion to prevent this dangerous situation.

Patterns of repression and destruction

Failing to achieve its plans in Kurdistan, the AKP government has turned the 'state of emergency' into an excellent opportunity to increase attacks on the Kurds. In sharp violation of the rules of war, the government has demolished the Kurdish towns of Cizre, Sur, Nusaybin, Idil, Gever, Silvan and Sirnak, during which process they massacred hundreds of people, forcing 1.5 million to migrate. In addition, in Cizre they burnt 103 civilians alive. In addition, they increased attacks on Kurdish legal politics and political representatives. Among those arrested are HDP co-chairs Selahattin Demirtas and Figen Yuksekdag, DBP co-chair Sebahat Tuncel, KJA spokesperson Ayla Akat Ata, and Amed Municipality co-chairs Gulten Kisanak and Firat Anli. Also, many more municipality and council co-chairs, Central Executive Board and Party Council and party members have been arrested. Therefore, the EUTCC conference:

- Calls for the immediate release of all political prisoners including the HDP co-chairs.
- Calls upon the state to withdraw all trustees and release the co-mayors and other deputies

Purging the Kurds and the opposition

After the coup attempt, Erdogan declared a state of emergency and purged all alleged and real opposition, turning Turkey into a vast prison. As the European Parliament noted, '[…] whereas these measures are disproportionate and in breach of basic rights and freedoms protected by the Turkish Constitution, of democratic values upon which the EU is founded and of the ICCPR; whereas the authorities have arrested 10 HDP deputies and some 150 journalists (the largest number worldwide); whereas 2,386 judges and prosecutors and 40,000 others are detained; whereas 129,000 public employees either remain suspended (66,000) or dismissed (63,000), most of whom had no charges brought against them.' Furthermore, 7 newspapers, 1 magazine, 1 radio station, and 375 associations have been closed down. In addition, 34 Kurdish mayors have been arrested while 57 municipalities in Kurdish areas have been replaced by the government's appointed trustees. Turkey's chief goal behind this wholesale purge is to ensure that the HDP will not pass the election threshold in the upcoming election. Therefore, the EUTCC conference:

- Calls upon Turkey to cease all the attacks on Kurds, the opposition, journalists, students and trade unionists, and to remove the prohibitions on the NGO, newspapers, radio stations, magazines and TV stations.

EU values

The fact that human rights and fundamental freedoms are the very heart of the EU is expressed in The Universal Declaration of Human Rights. Especially in the preamble the values of peace, human dignity and fundamental freedoms are mentioned as crucial values of the UN and EU. The simple reality is that Turkey is publicly and unashamedly violating all of this. There is no peace as terrorism and even war is imposed on the Kurds. Freedom of press, expression or religion are violated as mentioned by UN Special Rapporteur, United Nations High Commissioner for Human Rights, Amnesty International, and Human Rights Watch.

We call on the European Union, the Council of Europe and the United Nations:

- To support democratic forces and new democratic society models for peace in the Middle East;
- to acknowledge the Democratic Self-Administration of Rojava;
- to acknowledge and support the North Syria Federation;
- to start urgent Humanitarian Aid for the, from IS, liberated region in close co-operation with the local administration in Rojava;
- to take prompt action to halt the ongoing political coup taking place in Turkey;
- to follow up their statements of concern about developments in Turkey with decisive and effective measures.

We call on the European Union and the European governments:

To freeze the accession process with Turkey until President Erdogan begins to reverse his attacks on democracy, clamping down on civil and political rights, the shutting down of political organisations and the arrests of hundreds of thousands of people;

- To make it absolutely clear to Erdogan that his suspension of democracy and repression of democratic political opposition must cease immediately;
- to call for the release of all elected politicians, MPs and mayors of the HDP and other parties, who have been detained in the present clampdown, and to reinstate them to the posts to which they were legitimately elected;
- to signal its opposition by withdrawing embassy staff from Turkey to

demonstrate clearly that the present authoritarian politics of Erdogan are totally unacceptable;

- to take all the necessary measures to ensure that full democracy and civil rights are restored in Turkey;
- to make it clear to Turkey's political leaders that their current course poses a great danger to their own country by making it a pariah state, weakening its longstanding alliances and eroding its economic prosperity;
- to condemn strongly the discussion and the intention by the Turkish government to relaunch the death penalty;
- to send emergency delegations to visit the imprisoned MPs and mayors of the HDP.

The European Parliament 8 December, 2016

photo: Renaud Hoyois

Resistance on the ground

Angela Davis

President Trump's inauguration in January 2017 was swiftly followed by Women's Marches throughout the United States and more widely. Millions of people participated. Angela Davis caught the mood in Washington DC, in front of a crowd of hundreds of thousands. She has served as a juror on the Russell Tribunal on Palestine (see Spokesman 120*), and her book with Frank Barat,* Freedom is a Constant Struggle *(Haymarket 2016), is a bestseller.*

At a challenging moment in our history, let us remind ourselves that we the hundreds of thousands, the millions of women, trans-people, men and youth who are here at the Women's March, we represent the powerful forces of change that are determined to prevent the dying cultures of racism, hetero-patriarchy from rising again.

We recognise that we are collective agents of history and that history cannot be deleted like web pages. We know that we gather this afternoon on indigenous land and we follow the lead of the first peoples who, despite massive genocidal violence, have never relinquished the struggle for land, water, culture, their people. We especially salute today the Standing Rock Sioux.

The freedom struggles of black people that have shaped the very nature of this country's history cannot be deleted with the sweep of a hand. We cannot be made to forget that black lives do matter. This is a country anchored in slavery and colonialism, which means for better or for worse the very history of the United States is a history of immigration and enslavement. Spreading xenophobia, hurling accusations of murder and rape, and building walls will not erase history.

No human being is illegal.

The struggle to save the planet, to stop climate change, to guarantee the accessibility of water from the lands of the Standing Rock Sioux, to Flint, Michigan, to the West Bank and Gaza. The struggle to save our flora and fauna, to save the air – this is ground zero of the struggle for social justice.

This is a women's march and this

◄ *Angela Davis at Russell Tribunal on Palestine, Brussels, 2013* women's march represents the promise of feminism as against the pernicious powers of state violence; an inclusive and intersectional feminism that calls upon all of us to join the resistance to racism, to Islamophobia, to anti-Semitism, to misogyny, to capitalist exploitation.

Yes, we salute the fight for 15 [dollars an hour minimum wage]. We dedicate ourselves to collective resistance. Resistance to the billionaire mortgage profiteers and gentrifiers. Resistance to the health care privateers. Resistance to the attacks on Muslims and on immigrants. Resistance to attacks on disabled people. Resistance to state violence perpetrated by the police and through the prison industrial complex. Resistance to institutional and intimate gender violence, especially against trans women of colour.

Women's rights are human rights all over the planet and that is why we say freedom and justice for Palestine. We celebrate the impending release of Chelsea Manning. And Oscar López Rivera. But we also say free Leonard Peltier. Free Mumia Abu-Jamal. Free Assata Shakur.

Over the next months and years we will be called upon to intensify our demands for social justice, to become more militant in our defence of vulnerable populations. Those who still defend the supremacy of white male hetero-patriarchy had better watch out.

The next 1,459 days of the Trump administration will be 1,459 days of resistance: Resistance on the ground, resistance in the classrooms, resistance on the job, resistance in our art and in our music.

This is just the beginning and, in the words of the inimitable Ella Baker, 'we who believe in freedom cannot rest until it comes.'

www.russelltribunalonpalestine.com

Pax Americana
(Six haiku)

The Latest Demagogue

Odd hair and orange
face – Trump's bluster and vile jibes
reek of Halloween

Coinage Of Power

The phrase 'Post-Truth' means
in democracies (so-called)
all feel free to lie

Dr Strangelove And Mr Trump

Can such things be – that
perfect farce casteth out fear
of Apocalypse?

Trumpus Imperator Novus

Bullying bigot,
if not yet Nero, accedes.
One reads Lucretius…

Emperor Trump Addresses The Intelligentsia
(CIA HQ, Langley, January 2017)

Rent-A-Crowd applauds
his wild rants – an absurdist
ploy, bolstering lies

Unreality Shows

Let the Trumpites blare!
Claques, cliques, klaxons, deafen truth,
make music for fools

Alexis Lykiard

Peter Hennessy
& James Jinks

THE SILENT DEEP

The Royal Navy Submarine Service since 1945

'Riveting, definitive, a tour de force'
Spectator

'Spellbinding ... unprecedented'
The Times

Silent mindset

Commander
Robert Green
Royal Navy (Ret'd)

Approaching 700 pages excluding chapter notes, *The Silent Deep* is a formidable read. Space restriction confines me to an overview, before outlining and discussing highlights selected for their current relevance. Well referenced, it is too detailed at times; but it is comprehensive, thoroughly readable, and captures the subject's ethos. In their preface, veteran historian of British government Peter Hennessy and James Jinks explain that, while not an official history, they have tried to bridge the divide between those submariners determined to sustain their profession's image as the 'silent service', and others who feel this has become counterproductive, especially with the Submarine Service facing an increasingly uncertain future.

The authors received unprecedented access. The introduction sets the consequent, often reverential tone, describing the Submariners' Association Annual Memorial Service at the National Submarine War Memorial a week before Remembrance Sunday. Hennessy then offers highlights from his diary while 'embedded' in the nuclear attack submarine (SSN) *HMS Tireless* for a 'Perisher' course of prospective Commanding Officers (COs). He revels in dramatising what it takes to command this most complex and demanding naval weapon system in such a hostile environment. In conversation with former US submariners, they admire the swashbuckling attitude encouraged among British COs: '… the Royal Navy's SSNs would take more risks…', because the RN has so few 'boats' (in-house jargon for submarines) compared to the US Navy. A

Commander Green is a former operator of nuclear weapons.

French submariner goes further: 'French COs are more scientific. They are all engineers. The Royal Navy are more warriors.'

After World War Two, the Submarine Service had to cope with huge cuts in hulls and personnel while struggling to modernise submarine design. One revelation is the central role of Helmut Walter, the German scientist behind many of the revolutionary improvements in U-boat effectiveness.

It was an exciting time to be in submarines. The Cold War meant training to oppose the new Soviet threat by enforcing blockade of their waters where surface ships were too vulnerable, and to perform dangerous, uncomfortable covert reconnaissance missions. This required new skills and equipment associated with submarine-to-submarine combat, of which there had been almost no experience in World War Two. Emphasis shifted to high endurance and quiet running, with streamlining, stronger pressure hulls to permit deeper diving, plus extra pressure hull length to accommodate more batteries and motors. Development of new passive sonars, fire control equipment and torpedoes encountered many difficulties.

1956 saw the launch of *HMS Porpoise*, the first post-war conventional hunter-killer submarine (SSK), which was quieter than even the US equivalent *Guppy* class. However, the Americans were forging ahead with their prototype SSN *USS Nautilus*. The authors emphasise how Admiral of the Fleet Lord Louis Mountbatten overcame UK resistance to nuclear propulsion, competing with nuclear weapons and electricity generation. On becoming First Sea Lord in 1955, he masterminded getting alongside the USN, and charmed irascible Admiral Hyman Rickover, the all-powerful director of the highly secret US nuclear programme, into allowing *Nautilus* to show her paces in a major UK anti-submarine warfare (ASW) exercise. The RN realised it had to build nuclear submarines; thus the unequal struggle began to keep up with US and Soviet developments. Also, the need for effective ASW weapons precipitated an expedient, misguided drive for nuclear warheads. These would have been suicidal for the user and first alerted me, as Senior Observer of an ASW helicopter squadron equipped with nuclear depth bombs, to their military uselessness.

Mountbatten persuaded Rickover to visit UK, who advised buying the latest version of a nuclear propulsion plant, fitted in the newest SSN *USS Skipjack*, from Westinghouse via Rolls-Royce. This resulted in the US and UK signing the top secret 1958 agreement for 'Co-operation on the Uses of Atomic Energy for Mutual Defense Purposes', which with amendments remains in force.

Dreadnought was launched on Trafalgar Day, 21 October 1960, and her reactor went critical in November 1962, with sea trials completed by the end of the year. Lack of experience plus complicated improvements meant it took another four years before the second UK SSN, *HMS Valiant*, became operational. Another, *HMS Warspite*, followed; and a 'Repeat Valiant' class (*Churchill*, *Conqueror* and *Courageous*) appeared between 1970-71.

The authors recount the background to the UK's loss of Empire craving for a scaled down version of the US Polaris nuclear-armed ballistic missile submarine (SSBN). In the humiliating 1962 Nassau negotiations, Kennedy understandably tried to end the UK's independent nuclear status. As a face-saving ploy to avert the biggest crisis in the 'special relationship', Macmillan agreed to UK Polaris assignment to NATO except where 'supreme national interests' were at stake; but this was not credible. Implications for the RN were barely considered, for what would be the largest project since World War Two.

Four Polaris SSBNs were built almost to schedule, but imposed a huge strain on both shipbuilders and the Submarine Service. Pressure for a fifth boat arose from learning that the French were independently building five, the optimum for sustaining two on patrol. This prompted what the UK's leading exponent of nuclear deterrence, Sir Michael Quinlan, dubbed 'the national gut feeling': fear that France would have a superior nuclear force, which persists to this day. A fifth boat was approved in early 1964. Labour, under Wilson, rightly mocked the claim of UK Polaris independence; and it was an election issue in October 1964, with Labour pledging to renegotiate the Nassau Agreement.

The Labour government was left with serious economic problems; but Wilson and Denis Healey, Defence Secretary, were quickly persuaded to continue with Polaris. Wilson justified it as 'having a handle on the Americans'; but as always in the history of the 'special relationship', the reverse was true.

The authors record some interesting comments from former Polaris COs about their appalling responsibility. These ranged widely, from prayerful reliance on not receiving a firing order in the hope that nuclear deterrence would always work, through indifference driven by the professional imperative to present a credible threat (plus the let-out that Polaris was a second strike system), to several prospective commanding officers turning down the prestigious appointment, effectively ending their careers.

The SSK development story resumes with introduction of the *Oberon* class, of which 13 were built between 1961-67. Quieter than the *Porpoise* class, they could dive deeper and had better detection equipment; but both classes were considered highly effective.

The 1966 Labour Defence White Paper cancelling CVA-01, a new class of strike aircraft carrier, meant a major re-orientation of the Royal Navy to anti-submarine warfare. The nuclear powered attack submarine (SSN) was promoted as the future capital ship, and protection of deploying nuclear-armed submarines from Soviet detection and trailing ('delousing') became a new essential role. The US Navy and Royal Navy began more aggressive operations, collecting intelligence and shadowing Soviet SSNs as a form of controlled confrontation. Passive sonar gave only a bearing, not range or depth. This risked collision, at least one of which occurred, luckily with only minor damage; and there were numerous near-misses.

The new *Swiftsure* SSN class (six commissioned from 1973) had increased diving depth, and retractable forward hydroplanes making them quieter, helped by pumpjet propulsion, which explained the slight stern bulge, and was so successful that all subsequent nuclear powered attack submarines were given it. Computerised tactical data handling and fire control systems were a huge advance; but weapon problems persisted until recently.

Torpedo limitations resulted in the commanding officer of *HMS Conqueror* falling back on World War Two design Mk8 torpedoes to controversially sink the Argentine cruiser *General Belgrano* in the 1982 Falklands War. A chapter is devoted to this first war experience for UK SSNs. With only seven nuclear powered attack submarines available, establishing early barriers around the Falklands, and then maintaining them, proved challenging. As I discovered as Staff Officer (Intelligence) to CINCFLEET, there was little information about the Argentine conventional submarine threat (two ex-US *Guppy* class, and two modern German Type 209 class); but the latter were known to be quiet, and posed a serious potential threat to the Task Force and nuclear-powered attack submarines.

Frustrations grew when bad weather, associated poor sonar detection conditions, and shallow water limitations resulted in fleeting surface contacts, exacerbated by slow communications and initially restrictive rules of engagement. *Splendid* developed an electrical generator fault, forcing her to withdraw under diesel power in a storm; unable to snort, she nearly ran out of battery power, and was replaced by *Courageous*. *Valiant* arrived struggling with defects; and *Conqueror*'s communication problems intensified after a trailing wire aerial became wrapped round her screw. Heroic efforts by a diver removed enough to enable her to stay operational, and return home to an unsurprisingly subdued welcome.

The intriguing rumour of nuclear-armed submarine deployment south in case UK forces faced defeat is probed; but the commanding officer of the deployed boat, *HMS Resolution*, received no such order. However, the possibility of an extremely secret contingency plan re-emerged in the 2005 memoirs of Ali Magoudi, French President Mitterrand's psychoanalyst. He recounted a chilling phone call from Mrs Thatcher after a French-supplied Exocet missile fired by a French-supplied Super Étendard naval strike jet crippled the destroyer *HMS Sheffield* in retaliation for loss of the *Belgrano*. Apparently, the British Prime Minister threatened a nuclear strike against Argentina unless Mitterrand informed her of the frequency of the Exocet target acquisition system; and he was so convinced of her seriousness that he complied. Sir Lawrence Freedman's official history of the Falklands campaign claims that 'the nuclear option was never seriously discussed…'; but Quinlan confirmed that Thatcher did consider use of nuclear weapons in extreme circumstances: '…she took it very seriously…'. For me, this highlighted the danger of a leader of a nuclear-armed state facing defeat, especially against a non-nuclear state. Had the commanding officer of a nuclear-armed submarine received such an order and obeyed, the failure of nuclear deterrence would have compounded the ignominy of defeat with that of being the first to have broken the nuclear taboo since Nagasaki.

As expected, the authors display a sure touch covering the extremely secret and costly 1970s Chevaline programme to shore up the credibility of UK Polaris against Moscow's anti-ballistic missile (ABM) defences, and replacement with Trident. Building four *Vanguard* class Trident SSBNs and support facilities in the Clyde Submarine Base at Faslane was the largest, most complex and expensive construction programme in Western Europe.

The Royal Navy's decisive role in salvaging Mr Thatcher's career – before the Falklands War she was the most unpopular Prime Minister in history – restored a few surface ship cuts in the 1981 defence review. The Type 2400 *Upholder* SSK class, initially costing a third of that of an SSN, was a less demanding way to lift submarine numbers. Following delays and increased costs, *Upholder* was delivered in 1990; three more followed.

Meanwhile, the first of seven successor SSNs to the *Swiftsure* class, *HMS Trafalgar*, launched in 1981, was quieter still, with improved passive sonar and fire control systems. The late 1980s 'were the glory days of the Submarine Service'. However, nuclear-powered attack submarines were effectively seconded to the US Navy; and many submariners felt detached from the rest of the Royal Navy, who had no idea what they were up to. SSN commanding officers reminisced about how exciting it was to 'win' the Cold War; but maybe they should be grateful for Soviet restraint under provocation in their backyard?

The 'glory days' were short-lived. A month after the Berlin Wall came down, in 1989, cracks were found in *Warspite*'s propulsion system pipe welds. All *Valiant* and *Swiftsure* SSNs had to be recalled for complicated repairs, and the nuclear-armed submarines struggled to keep one on patrol despite weld cracks being found in them. Operational commitments overloaded the *Trafalgar* class, and mistakes were made. A 1990 defence review cut 27 SSNs and SSKs by almost half, including the entire new *Upholder* SSK class. Widespread anger at this ensued because of the loss of important command experience, and appalling waste of money and skills. They were eventually sold to the Canadians as replacements for their *Oberon* class. The authors fail to ask if this was the opportunity cost of getting Trident? Also, the first Gulf War in 1991 is not mentioned, presumably because SSNs had no role in the shallow waters, two *Oberon* class SSKs being preferred for Special Forces operations.

With *Vanguard* and *Victorious* operational, Polaris was stood down in August 1996 after 28 years. Two years later, the Blair Government announced that by 2006 the submarine fleet would be cut to 10 SSNs and 4 SSBNs.

From the mid-1990s the SSN role began to shift to power projection. Purchase of US Tomahawk land attack (TLAM) cruise missiles in 1995 enabled them to catch up with the US SSN land attack capability first demonstrated in the 1991 Gulf War. The first UK SSN fitted with them, *Splendid*, saw action in the 1999 NATO war against Serbia. The *Trafalgar* class followed, integrated into US forces in the Gulf and Mediterranean.

In April 2001, the Submarine Service celebrated its centenary, overshadowed by increasing overstretch and a new propulsion system crisis. A serious generic design/manufacturing fault had been found in the primary cooling circuit of *Tireless*; repairs took a year. Two UK SSNs fired TLAM against Afghanistan targets in 2001; and two (with 12 US ones) took part in the 2003 invasion of Iraq. Long deployments in warm waters took a toll on the often cutting edge technology, while SSN service life had to be extended from 25 to 33 years. In 2011, two SSNs participated in NATO's Libyan campaign, conducting close-in intelligence gathering and firing Tomahawk cruise missiles. The last of the *Swiftsure* class had to be scrapped in 2010; and delays to the new *Astute* SSN class meant that, in 2012, *Turbulent* went, leaving five nuclear-powered attack submarines barely able to sustain SSBN delousing and Perisher training, let alone anti-submarine warfare exercising.

The sad saga of the *Astute* programme highlights anxieties about a viable future for the Submarine Service. In 2002, *Astute*'s construction was three years behind and several hundred million over budget: 200 US designers and managers, including a new project director, had to be brought in to help. Launched in 2007, problems abounded, including design flaws, unreliable equipment and poor construction; and her cost had rocketed to almost £1.4bn. Soon after commissioning in 2010, *Astute* ran aground; then a disaffected sailor shot dead one officer and injured another. The Royal Navy pleaded that all issues had been addressed, and she was 50 per cent quieter than the *Trafalgar* class.

Seven *Astute* class are being built, the last planned to enter service in 2024; so most of the surviving four *Trafalgar* class will need to remain in service until then and *Astute* boats be worked harder, or reduce commitments. A recruiting crisis has led to a shortage in engineers and younger officers, and allowing women in submarines. There is fear of a serious, unconcealable nuclear accident, which could 'be the end of the Submarine Service'. The worst such accident yet was the farcical 2009 collision between *Vanguard* submerged on 'deterrent' patrol and the French patrolling SSBN *Le Triomphant*, miraculously causing only minor mutual damage. This is described without any discussion of the appalling implications.

The last chapter of *The Silent Deep* covers the 'Successor' SSBN programme (recently reviving the name *Dreadnought*), final Parliamentary approval for which was given on 18 July 2016. Blair conceded in his 2010 memoirs the commonsense and practical arguments against Trident renewal, including huge expense for no military use; but so far the perceived loss of status, not least relating to the French, has prevailed.

The new SSBN design incorporates a Common Missile Compartment (CMC) with that planned in the US *Ohio* class SSBN replacement (to be named *Columbia*), the programme for which has just been approved. It is unprecedented for the Royal Navy to be planning to build it first. Because of delays in the UK decision, the *Vanguard* class service life has to be extended to 37 years. Running them on for 6-8 years longer than the *Resolution* class is another leap in the dark, as is getting *Dreadnought* into service by the early 2030s until possibly the 2060s. Again, US know-how and personnel are indispensable; the highest grade steel has to come from French monopoly suppliers, and costs have already grown to £31bn. Yet the authors remain chipper that it will happen, citing Cicero that 'the safety of the people is the chief law'. However, this could be turned on its head by the staunchly anti-nuclear Labour leader, Jeremy Corbyn.

A disconcerting epilogue opens by returning to *HMS Tireless*, eulogising her recent decommissioning, joining 18 other nuclear submarines awaiting dismantling. With *Dreadnought* rusting in Rosyth since 1980, the cost of maintaining them is rising and space running out as the Ministry of Defence struggles to find an environmentally safe and cost-effective means of disposal. In a poignant ending, the authors confront the reality that the Submarine Service's 'glory days' are leaving a dark, irresponsible legacy of still unresolved radioactive contamination, and a barely viable surface Fleet.

As the UK government and Royal Navy anxiously persist with the increasingly vulnerable *Astute* and new *Dreadnought* programmes, I found this book – with its photos, illustrations of past and present submarines, decode of acronyms, and detailed maps of the Falklands campaign – valuable in understanding what lies behind their mindset.

Peter Hennessy & James Jinks, The Silent Deep: The Royal Navy Submarine Service since 1945, Penguin Books, 2016, paperback ISBN 9780241959480, £12.99

* * *

Ageing Trident

In June 2016, following a major refit, the British nuclear armed submarine HMS Vengeance *attempted to fire a Trident missile without its nuclear warheads. The submarine and crew passed muster, but the Trident missile veered off course, apparently towards the coast of the United States, before it was destroyed.*

According to the US Department of Defence, the Trident II D5 missile has completed its 26th year of deployment and 'has reached its original design life goal'. As the DoD commented, 'like any other ageing weapon system, increased maintenance and repair will be required to sustain a safe, reliable and accurate strategic weapons system'. The DoD also notes that the 'US Navy has been actively engaging with the company to "aggressively lower" the amount of money it spends maintaining Trident'. The failed test was kept secret from the public, although Theresa May, newly appointed UK Prime Minister, was informed. She neglected to inform MPs of the failure when, weeks later, Parliament was asked to approve the construction of four successor Dreadnought *class submarines to carry the ageing missiles. The budget for the new submarines runs to tens of billions of pounds.*

The Spokesman *asked Hans M Kristensen of the Federation of American Scientists, who has followed the Trident programme for years (see Spokesman 127), to comment. He said:*

'All missiles wear out as they age. But Trident II D5 is by far the most reliable long-range ballistic missile in the world. The Trident II D5 as it was originally designed is reaching the end of its life so the US Navy has been developing a life-extended version over the past decade-plus that will begin deploying this year: Trident II D5LE (LE stands for life extended). The LE will completely replace the older versions on US SSBNs and will also arm the new British SSBNs. The LE version is designed to last through the 2040s. The US Navy is in the early stages of designing a replacement for the LE version that will probably be back-fitted onto US and British SSBNs in the 2040s.

A general reminder about the purpose of missile flight-testing programmes. Their purpose is to detect problems so they can be fixed. Every flight test finds "issues" that are then addressed. It is the cumulative findings and fixes that enable the Trident to be as repairable as it is. So a few failures over time doesn't necessarily indicate a reliability problem; but a series of failures over a short period would certainly do so.'

When asked whether it was the life-extended version of Trident that Vengeance *tested, Hans replied:*

'That is likely, but I don't know for sure. The US Navy has been testing the LE version for several years, including DASO [Demonstration and Shakedown Operation] events like the British post-refuelling test last June. The LE has the new guidance system, the Mk6, developed by Draper. So it's possible we're seeing the preparation for the introduction of the LE on British SSBNs. The warhead section on the British missiles has already been upgraded with the new Mk4A re-entry body that provide a significantly enhanced target kill capability; it gives the British SSBNs hard-target kill capability.'

Hans M. Kristensen is Director of the Nuclear Information Project at the Federation of American Scientists in Washington, DC. He is co-author of the bi-monthly FAS Nuclear Notebook column in the Bulletin of the Atomic Scientists *and the World Nuclear Forces overview in the* SIPRI Yearbook, *and is a frequent advisor to the news media on the status of nuclear forces and policy.*

SIPRI Yearbook 2016: Armaments, Disarmament and International Security (Oxford University Press ISBN 9780198787280, £100)

THE SPOKESMAN

Become a subscriber…

Subscription rates (for four issues):

Individual subscriptions UK £20

Individual subscriptions – international £25

Institutional subscriptions
UK -- £33 Europe -- £38 RoW -- £40

Please send me one year's subscription, starting with Issue No. ____

I enclose payment of £ ____

Name ______________________________

Address ____________________________

____

_____________ Postcode ____________

Please return this form [a copy will do] with a cheque or money order made payable to 'Bertrand Russell House'. Send to The Spokesman, Russell House, Bulwell Lane, Nottingham, NG6 0BT, England.

Payments can be made online -- please visit www.spokesmanbook.com

Prevent nuclear catastrophe

A policy proposal

Caroline Leroy

The author is a Politics and International Relations student at the University of Bath who is currently on work placement with Parliamentarians for Nuclear Non-Proliferation and Disarmament (PNND) in Basel, Switzerland. Her essay won first prize of £500 in the 2017 Student/Young Pugwash (SYP) blog-writing competition, which asked participants to 'imagine you are advising the UK government about ways to decrease the global threat of weapons of mass destruction. In approximately 1000 words, explain a policy, technique or approach that can reduce the threat(s) and make the world at least a bit safer'.

An alarming situation threatening the world is indicated by thousands of deployed nuclear weapons currently on high alert, especially as tensions increase between nuclear-armed states. Not only do these weapons pose a massive risk to human life; their use would likely constitute a major violation of international law, as affirmed by the International Court of Justice (ICJ). Nevertheless, many nuclear-armed states retain the option to use these weapons in an unspecified variety of ways and implicitly challenge key principles of international law. The United Kingdom, as one of nine nuclear-armed states, is in a position to push back and take a significant and influential step in strengthening the norm against any use of nuclear weapons. I argue for the UK to adopt a *no-first-use policy* which, I believe, will make the world safer in important and immediate ways.

In order to advance a proposal that has a possibility of being adopted by the UK government, it is important to understand the role that nuclear weapons have in British security strategy. By affirming that 'defence and protection start with deterrence' the UK government has made clear that it is not yet ready to phase out nuclear weapons entirely from its security doctrine. None the less, it has adopted a number of measures reducing the role of nuclear weapons and their readiness for use. For instance, it cut by half the number of nuclear warheads, and changed from minutes to days the 'notice to fire' on ballistic missile submarines on patrol, among others measures.

If the UK is interested in furthering its commitment to a safer world, it could adopt a *no-first-use policy* without undermining continued nuclear deterrence. This policy has already been adopted by India and China. If the UK embraced no-first-use, it would be able (along with China) to encourage other Permanent 5 members of the UN Security Council to follow suit, as well as use its position within NATO to influence certain key states. This is a diplomatic power neither China nor India possess. Indeed, the Obama Administration demonstrated an interest in the United States moving to no-first-use but indicated as a barrier the lack of support of some NATO allies, to whom 'extended nuclear deterrence' is provided. Yet, as an initial step, President Obama affirmed in the 2010 Nuclear Posture Review a 'primary purpose' of nuclear weapons being to deter only a nuclear strike from an aggressor, with the commitment to adopting a policy of deterrence against nuclear attack the 'sole purpose of their nuclear arsenal'.

This policy shift by the United States, along with increased international attention to the humanitarian consequences of any use of nuclear weapons, provides fertile ground for the United Kingdom to adopt no-first-use. In addition, the decision by the United Nations General Assembly to commence, in 2017, multilateral negotiations on a treaty to prohibit nuclear weapons places pressure on the nuclear-armed states to respond with a significant measure in the direction of disarmament, and possibly announce or adopt this at the UN High Level Conference on Nuclear Disarmament which will be held in 2018. No-first-use could be that measure.

Employing this policy could greatly improve not only national but also global security. To begin with, no-first-use would give Parliament a guarantee that a nuclear strike would not be authorised by the Prime Minister under the auspices of Royal Prerogative, unless the country has been attacked. First use of nuclear weapons constitutes a major act of war; a decision that should not be taken without democratic oversight. By ensuring that the Prime Minister could not authorise first use of nuclear weapons, Members of Parliament would protect democracy and their constituents' right to live in peace. This is particularly important in light of the Constitutional Reform and Governance Act 2010, which originally included a section on parliamentary approval required for the use of armed force, but this was dropped from the bill before it received royal assent.

Some security analysts might argue that no-first-use would undermine the ability of the UK to deter nuclear attacks by another nuclear-armed state. However, this is unconvincing given that the British nuclear arsenal is 'effectively invulnerable to pre-emptive attack' and is deployed using stealthy, nuclear-powered submarines. In the case of a nuclear attack on

British soil, the remaining nuclear force would be able to deliver a response with a significant, devastating blow to the aggressor.

Moreover, the UK also controls a powerful conventional military complex, the employment of which can conform to international law and morality, unlike the use of nuclear weapons. Indeed, since 1996 and the International Court of Justice's advisory opinion confirming the general illegality of use of nuclear weapons, there have been considerable developments in understanding the catastrophic humanitarian impact of any use of nuclear weapons, and of law protecting civilians, the environment and future generations. As such, it is irrefutable that any use of nuclear weapons would be illegal – and first use all the more so. It is likely that these developments influenced the Leader of the Opposition in the UK to affirm that, if he became Prime Minister, he would not push the button.

Adopting no-first-use would be a significant move that could bolster the UN Security Council Permanent Five (P5) Process initiated by the UK seven years ago, and make up for lack of progress so far. This is because British no-first-use policy would reduce the risk of nuclear catastrophe, triggering confidence-building measures amongst nuclear-armed states, reducing tensions that are reckoned to be at their highest since the Cold War. No-first-use impedes nuclear escalation that might result from such weapons being employed in a conventional military conflict as a result of such increased tensions, particularly between the West and Russia. In addition, Britain could positively influence the upcoming Nuclear Posture Review under the Trump Presidency, after no-first-use received strong support during the final year of the Obama Administration.

Finally, nuclear weapons pose a huge threat to our world. The UK could show leadership by reducing the role that such weapons play in security doctrines. This would challenge the dangerous Cold War-era reasoning that has re-emerged and help decrease tensions between nuclear-armed states. There is no doubt that a nuclear-weapon-free world would be much safer, but this seems unattainable in the short term. A no-first-use policy bridges this long-term goal with a feasible action that the UK could take *now* to reduce the likelihood of a nuclear catastrophe and build greater security.

References available on request.

syp@britishpugwash.org
www.britishpugwash.org

Spokesman Books

Publishing imprint of the **Bertrand Russell Peace Foundation**

RECENT TITLES

Dawn of the Unread

When the dead go unread ... There's gonna be trouble

Editor: James Walker | Art: Paul Fillingham
Assisted by Adrian Reynolds and Wayne Burrows

Dawn of the Unread imagines a scenario whereby dead writers from Nottingham's past are incensed at the closures of libraries and low literacy levels in 21st Century Britain. Sillitoe, Lawrence, Byron et al would never put up with such an insult and so return from the grave, in a twist on the zombie genre, in search of the one thing that will ensure their survival: 'boooks'.

Price: £14.99 ISBN: 978 0 85124 8592

Climate of Peace?

The Spokesman 134
Edited by Tony Simpson

Alva White - We rescue people
Tony Simpson - The Conflict Shoreline
Jeremy Corbyn MP - Environment and Energy
Nick Buxton - Securing whose future?
Maria Sotiropoulou - Cruel Sea
Reiner Hoffman - Sustainable Development
John Pilger - Finish Line
Bertrand Russell - Pugwash Point of View

Price: £6 ISBN: 978 0 85124 8622

Architect or Bee? The Human Price of Technology

By Mike Cooley, Foreword by Frances O'Grady

Mike Cooley's pioneering introduction to socially useful production and human-centred manufacturing systems, with a new foreword by the General Secretary of the TUC, herself an advocate of the lessons of the Lucas Plan for alternative production priorities. Years ahead of its time, *Architect or Bee?* is essential reading for all those seeking a democratic alternative to the politics of austerity.

Price: £10.99 ISBN: 978 0 85124 8493

www.spokesmanbooks.com

Delicious soup

Xi Jinping

In January 2017, Chinese President Xi Jinping addressed the United Nations in Geneva, in the presence of António Guterres, the UN's new Secretary-General. We reprint excerpts from President Xi's wide-ranging speech. Its global approach to peace and development, and its call for a world free of nuclear weapons, strike more positive notes during turbulent times.

… When countries enjoy peace, so will the world; when countries fight, the world suffers. From the Peloponnesian War in the fifth century BC to the two world wars and the Cold War that lasted more than four decades, we have drawn painful and profound lessons. 'History, if not forgotten, can serve as a guide for the future.' By establishing the United Nations, those before us won more than 70 years of relative peace for the world. What we need to do is to improve the mechanisms and means to more effectively resolve disputes, reduce tension, and put an end to wars and conflicts.

The Swiss writer and Nobel laureate Hermann Hesse stressed the importance of serving 'not war and destruction but peace and reconciliation'. Countries should foster partnerships based on dialogue, non-confrontation and non-alliance. Major powers should respect each other's core interests and major concerns, keep their differences under control, and build a new model of relations featuring non-conflict, non-confrontation, mutual respect and win-win co-operation. As long as we maintain communication and treat each other with sincerity, the 'Thucydides trap' can be avoided. Big countries should treat smaller ones as equals, instead of acting as a hegemon imposing their will on others. No country should open the Pandora's box by wilfully waging wars or undermining the international rule of law. **Nuclear weapons, the Sword of Damocles that hangs over mankind, should be completely prohibited and thoroughly destroyed over time to make the world free of nuclear weapons.** Guided by the principle of peace, sovereignty, inclusiveness and shared governance, we should turn the deep sea, the polar regions, outer space and the Internet into new frontiers for co-operation, rather than a wrestling ground for competition.

We should build a world of common security for all through joint efforts. No country in the world can enjoy absolute security. A country cannot have security while others are in turmoil, as threats facing other countries may haunt it also. When neighbours are in trouble, instead of tightening one's own fences, one should extend a helping hand to them. As the saying goes, 'united we stand, divided we fall'. All countries should pursue common, comprehensive, co-operative and sustainable security.

Terrorist attacks in Europe, North Africa and the Middle East in recent years once again demonstrate that terrorism is the common enemy of mankind. Fighting terrorism is the shared responsibility of all countries. In fighting terror, we should not just treat the symptoms, but remove its root causes. We should enhance co-ordination and build a global united front against terrorism so as to create an umbrella of security for people around the world.

The number of refugees has hit a record high since the end of the Second World War. While tackling the crisis, we should also get to its roots. Why would anyone want to be displaced if they have a home to return to? The UN High Commissioner for Refugees and the International Organization for Migration should act as the co-ordinators to mobilize the whole world to respond effectively to the refugee crisis. China has decided to provide an additional 200 million yuan of humanitarian assistance for refugees and the displaced of Syria.

As terrorism and refugee crises are closely linked to geopolitical conflicts, resolving conflicts provides the fundamental solution to such problems. Parties directly involved should return to the negotiating table, and other parties should work to facilitate talks for peace, and we should all respect the role the UN plays as the main channel for mediation.

Pandemic diseases such as bird flu, Ebola and Zika have sounded the alarm for international health security. The World Health Organization should play a leadership role in strengthening epidemic monitoring and sharing of information, practices and technologies. The international community should step up support and assistance for public health in African countries and other developing countries.

We should build a world of common prosperity through win-win co-operation. Development is the top priority for all countries. Instead of beggaring thy neighbour, countries should stick together like passengers in the same boat. All countries, the main economies in particular, should strengthen macro policy co-ordination, pursue both current and long-term interests, and focus on resolving deep-seated problems. We should seize the historic opportunity presented by a new round of the scientific and technological revolution and industrial transformation, shift growth models, drive growth through innovation, and further unleash social productivity and social creativity. We should uphold World Trade Organization rules, support an open, transparent, inclusive and non-discriminatory multilateral trading regime, and build an open world economy. Trade protectionism and self-isolation will benefit no one.

Economic globalization, a surging historical trend, has greatly facilitated trade, investment, flow of people, and technological advances. Since the turn of the century, under the auspices of the UN and riding on the waves of economic globalization, the international community has set the Millennium Development Goals and the 2030 Agenda for Sustainable Development. Thanks to these initiatives, 1.1 billion people have been lifted out of poverty, 1.9 billion people now have access to safe drinking water, 3.5 billion people have gained access to the Internet, and the goal has been set to eradicate extreme poverty by 2030. All this demonstrates that economic globalization is moving in the right direction. Of course, challenges such as development disparity, governance dilemmas, digital divide, and equity deficit still exist. But they are growing pains. We should face these problems and tackle them, instead of taking no action. As we Chinese like to say, one should not stop eating for fear of getting choked.

We should draw inspiration from history. Historians told us long ago that rapid economic development makes social reform necessary; but people tend to support the former while rejecting the latter. Instead of watching in hesitation, we should move forward against all odds. Answers can also be found in reality. The 2008 international financial crisis teaches us that we should strengthen co-ordination and improve governance so as to ensure sound growth of economic globalization and make it open, inclusive, balanced and beneficial to all. We should make the cake bigger and share it fairly to ensure justice and equity.

In September 2016, the G20 Summit in Hangzhou focused on global economic governance and other major issues, adopted the 'Blueprint on Innovative Growth', put development in the global macro policy framework for the first time, and formulated an action plan.

We should build an open and inclusive world through exchanges and mutual learning. Delicious soup is made by combining different ingredients. Diversity of human civilizations not only defines our world, but also drives progress of mankind. There are more than 200 countries and regions, over 2,500 ethnic groups, and multiple religions in our world. Different histories, national conditions, ethnic groups and customs give birth to different civilizations and make our world a colourful one. There is no such thing as a superior or inferior civilization, and civilizations are different only in identity and location. Diversity of civilizations should not be a source of global conflict; rather, it should be an engine driving the advance of human civilizations.

Every civilization, with its own appeal and root, is a human treasure. Diverse civilizations should draw on each other to achieve common progress. We should make exchanges among civilizations a source of inspiration for advancing human society and a bond that keeps the world in peace.

We should make our world clean and beautiful by pursuing green and low-carbon development. Man coexists with nature, which means that any harm to nature will eventually come back to haunt man. We hardly notice natural resources such as air, water, soil and blue sky when we have them. But we won't be able to survive without them. Industrialization has created material wealth never seen before, but it has also inflicted irreparable damage to the environment. We must not exhaust all the resources passed on to us by previous generations and leave nothing to our children, or pursue development in a destructive way. Clear waters and green mountains are as good as mountains of gold and silver. We must maintain harmony between man and nature and pursue sustainable development.

We should pursue a green, low-carbon, circular and sustainable way of life and production, advance the 2030 Agenda for Sustainable Development in a balanced manner, and explore a model of sound development that ensures growth, better lives and a good environment. The Paris Agreement is a milestone in the history of climate governance. We must ensure this endeavour is not derailed. All parties should work together to implement the Paris Agreement. China will continue to take steps to tackle climate change and fully honour its obligations.

The Swiss army knife embodies Swiss craftsmanship. When I first got one, I was amazed that it has so many functions. I cannot help thinking how wonderful it would be if an exquisite Swiss army knife could be made for our world. When there is a problem, we can use one of the tools on the knife to fix it. I believe that with unremitting efforts of the international community, such a knife can be made.

For us Chinese, China will do well only when the world does well, and vice versa. Many people are quite interested in what policies China will pursue, and we have heard various views. Here, I wish to give you an explicit answer.

First, China remains unchanged in its commitment to uphold world peace. Amity with neighbours, harmony without uniformity, and peace are values cherished in Chinese culture. *The Art of War*, a Chinese classic, begins with this observation:

> 'The art of war is of vital importance to the State. It is a matter of life and death, a road to either survival or ruin. Hence it demands careful study.'

What it means is that every effort should be made to prevent a war and great caution must be exercised when it comes to fighting a war. For several millennia, peace has been in the blood of us Chinese and part of our DNA.

Several centuries ago, China was strong and its gross domestic product accounted for 30 per cent of the global total. Even then, China was never engaged in aggression or expansion. For more than 100 years after the 1840 Opium War, China suffered immensely from aggression, wars and chaos. Confucius said, 'do not do to others what you do not want others to do to you'. We Chinese firmly believe that peace and stability is the only way to development and prosperity.

China has grown from a poor and weak country to the world's second largest economy, not by committing military expansion or colonial plunder, but through the hard work of its people and our efforts to uphold peace. China will never waver in its pursuit of peaceful development. No matter how strong its economy grows, China will never seek hegemony, expansion or sphere of influence. History has borne this out and will continue to do so.

Second, China remains unchanged in its commitment to pursue common development. An old Chinese saying goes, when you reap fruits, you should remember the tree; when you drink water, you should remember its source. China's development has been possible because of the world, and China has contributed to the world's development. We will continue to pursue a win-win strategy of opening up, sharing our development opportunities with other countries, and welcoming them aboard the fast train of China's development.

Between 1950 and 2016, China provided foreign countries with over 400 billion yuan of aid, and we will continue to increase assistance to others as our ability permits. Since the outbreak of the international financial crisis, China has contributed to more than 30 per cent of global growth each year on average. In the coming five years, China will import eight trillion US dollars of goods, attract 600 billion US dollars of foreign investment, make 750 billion US dollars of outward investment, and Chinese tourists will make 700 million visits abroad. All this will bring more development opportunities to other countries.

China pursues a path of development in keeping with its national conditions. We always put people's rights and interests above everything else and have worked hard to advance and uphold human rights. China has met the basic living needs of its 1.3 billion-plus people and lifted over 700 million people out of poverty, which is a significant contribution to the global cause of human rights. The Belt and Road initiative I put forward aims to achieve win-win and shared development. Over 100 countries and international organizations have supported the initiative, and a large number of early harvest projects have been launched. China supports the successful operation of the Asian Infrastructure Investment Bank and other new multilateral financial institutions in order to provide more public goods to the international community.

Third, China remains unchanged in its commitment to foster partnerships. China pursues an independent foreign policy of peace, and is ready to enhance friendship and co-operation with all other countries on the basis of the Five Principles of Peaceful Co-existence. China is the first country to make partnership-building a principle guiding state-to-state relations. It has formed partnerships of various forms with over 90 countries and regional organizations, and will build a circle of friends across the world.

China will endeavour to put in place a framework of relations with major powers featuring general stability and balanced growth. We will strive to build a new model of major country relations with the United States, a comprehensive strategic partnership of co-ordination with Russia, partnership for peace, growth, and reform among different civilizations with Europe, and a partnership of unity and cooperation with BRICS countries [Brazil, Russia, India, China, South Africa]. China will continue to uphold justice and friendship and pursue shared interests, and boost pragmatic co-operation with other developing countries to achieve common development. We will further enhance mutually beneficial co-operation with our neighbours under the principle of amity, sincerity, mutual benefit and inclusiveness. We will pursue common development that is result oriented with African countries in a spirit of sincerity, affinity and good faith. And we will elevate our comprehensive co-operative partnership with Latin America to a higher level.

Fourth, China remains unchanged in its commitment to multilateralism. Multilateralism is an effective way to preserve peace and promote development. For decades, the United Nations and other international institutions have made a universally recognized contribution to maintaining global peace and sustaining development.

China is a founding member of the United Nations and the first country to put its signature to the UN Charter. China will firmly uphold the international system with the UN as its core, the basic norms governing international relations embodied in the purposes and principles of the UN Charter, the authority and stature of the UN, and its core role in international affairs.

The China-UN Peace and Development Fund has been inaugurated officially. We will make funds available to peace and development oriented programmes proposed by the UN and its agencies in Geneva on a priority basis. China's support for multilateralism will increase as the country continues to develop itself.

Geneva evokes a special memory for us. In 1954, Premier Zhou Enlai led a Chinese delegation to the Geneva Conference, and worked with the Soviet Union, the United States, the United Kingdom and France to seek political settlement of the Korean issue and a ceasefire in Indo-China. This demonstrated China's desire for peace and contributed Chinese wisdom to world peace. Since 1971, when China regained its lawful seat at the UN and began to return to international agencies in Geneva, China has gradually involved itself in disarmament, trade, development, human rights and social issues, putting forth Chinese proposals for the resolution of major issues and the making of important rules. In recent years, China has taken an active part in dialogues and negotiations on the Iranian nuclear issue, the Syrian and other hotspot issues, giving Chinese input to their political settlement. China applied to the International Olympic Committee to host both the summer and winter Olympic and Paralympic Games, and we have won the bids. In addition, we have gained endorsement from the International Union for Conservation of Nature for over a dozen applications for world natural heritage sites as well as world cultural and natural heritage sites. All this has presented Chinese splendour to the world.

The ancient Chinese believed that 'one should be good at finding the laws of things and solving problems'. Building a community of shared future is an exciting goal, and it requires efforts from generation after generation. China is ready to work with all the other UN member states as well as international organizations and agencies to advance the great cause of building a community of shared future for mankind.

On 28 January, we Chinese celebrate the Chinese New Year, the Year of the Rooster. The rooster symbolizes bright prospects and auspiciousness. As a Chinese saying goes, the crow of the golden rooster heralds a great day for all.

‘Gentil Knight’

Bruce Kent
and
Robert Hinde

Bruce Kent, apostle of peace, pays tribute to his friend, Robert Hinde.

With Robert’s death I have lost a great inspiration and a good friend. A former Master of St John’s College, Cambridge, his academic work was known worldwide. Ethology, primatology, psychology and anthropology — the list of his expertise, achievements and honours is a very long one. His output was amazing: more than 300 books, articles and speeches.

As a pilot in Coastal Command during World War Two, he spent years on Catalinas and Sunderlands searching the Atlantic for enemy submarines before he was sent, at the end of the war, to the Indian Ocean. It was a war that cost him a brother and another childhood friend.

It also turned his mind to the building of peace. This new direction put him in touch with a man who shared his hopes and vision. Professor Joseph Rotblat was the only scientist, as far as I know, who refused to continue working on the atomic bomb once he discovered how it was to be used. In the 1950s, Rotblat was one of the founders of Pugwash, the international group of scientists, working for a more peaceful world. It brought scientists together from both sides in the Cold War and other countries as well. Robert was Chair and, later, President of Pugwash.

I met him through the Movement for the Abolition of War, which was founded soon after the great peace gathering of 10,000 people in The Hague in 1999. Robert succeeded Joseph Rotblat as our President in 2008. He was very much an active member. He came regularly to committee meetings, and helped us to plan Remembrance Day events such as the lecture held annually at the Imperial War

Museum. When he could not come to London for such meetings we had them in his study at St John's.

Absolutely committed as a peacemaker he was not a pacifist, though he was never critical about the tactics or beliefs of others working in the same direction. Few of us knew the details of his distinguished academic career, nor did he ever make much of his wartime experiences. His personal modesty was, by the normal standards of self-importance, his outstanding weakness.

In the last period of his life Robert wrote a memoir entitled *My 'War'*, explaining how his worldview had changed. This sums up his approach:

> ' … efforts to abolish war must focus on the world view of the "man or woman in the street" – as indeed anti-war organisations are doing to an increasing extent. Changing the popular view of war as heroic, inevitable, or a solution to disputes must be an important strategy for peace.'

Soon I became more than just a partner in an organisation, but a personal friend, both of Robert and his ever-welcoming wife, Joan. When last I saw him he was very ill, lying in bed and looking out over his garden at the bird feeder. A great variety of birds came to squabble over it in their search for food. If he did not know them all personally, he certainly knew every species that turned up.

How to remember him? My mind goes back to school and the Prologue to Chaucer's *Canterbury Tales*. One of those pilgrims was the soldier. 'A verray parfit gentil Knight.' That was Robert. He will be greatly missed. His inspiration will live on in the hearts of all who knew and loved him.

* * *

Robert Hinde
1923-2016

From time to time, Robert Hinde would phone the Russell Foundation in Nottingham, usually when he had a new publication in mind. He last called in late 2016, to say that the shop at the Imperial War Museum was now stocking copies of *My 'War'*, a personal account of his 'post-war aversion to war' and an attempt to trace the origins of that aversion. *My 'War'* was the last of Professor Hinde's five titles which the Russell Foundation printed and published down the years.

The immediate stimulus for *My 'War'* was a family request to Robert to know what he had done during the Second World War. 'They will be disappointed by my boring tale,' he wrote. 'It is not exciting, and I am glad to say that I did not kill anyone and no one tried specifically to kill me.' Warming to his task, however, Robert saw the memoir as providing 'some material for reflecting on the ways in which experience might affect one's outlook on life'. In this approach, he seemed to echo that of Bertrand Russell who, a century earlier, had written and lectured on *Principles of Social Reconstruction* in an attempt to get to the root causes of the First World War, and to avoid its repetition.

A biologist and ornithologist by

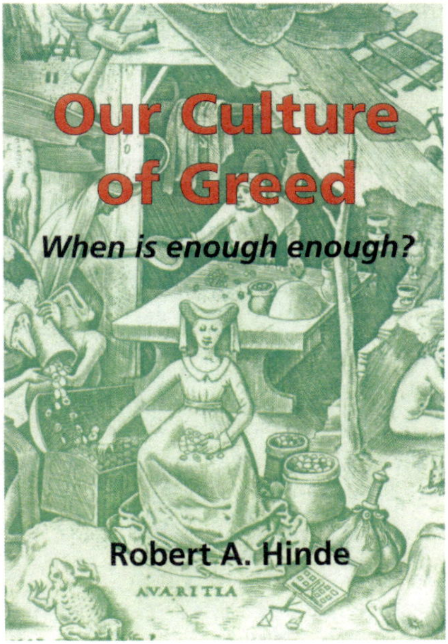

training, Robert was interested in 'understanding the nature of our morality' and its evolutionary implications. As such, he has been described as the 'grand old man of British ethology', defined as the 'scientific study of the function and evolution of animal behaviour patterns'. An excerpt from his book, *Changing How We Live* (Spokesman 2011), illustrates the point.

In December 2014, we visited Robert in his rooms at St John's College, Cambridge, to discuss the forthcoming publication of *Our Culture of Greed* (Spokesman 2015). Afterwards, with characteristic thoughtfulness and generosity, he provided a tour of the College, including its libraries, ancient and modern. He was particularly proud of the latter, which had been added during his tenure as Master of St John's.

Tony Simpson

* * *

Why one should be kind

… 'Selfish assertivesness' and 'prosociality' are shorthands, each for a variety of types of behaviour. Selfish assertiveness includes aggression, selfishness, greed, and so on. Prosociality includes helping, co-operation, sharing, loving and related behaviour. The two categories are useful for heuristic purposes though clearly heterogenous and the distinction breaks

down if pressed too far: how far they represent separate mechanisms is an open issue.

Prosociality requires emphasis. With the media reporting all sorts of horrors and brutal acts, and with the memory of the Holocaust, Hiroshima and Nagasaki still with us, it is easy to believe that evil is inevitable. A slick statement like 'to put it bluntly, all life on earth is based on selfishness' requires to be carefully picked apart before it is misunderstood. At the ultimate evolutionary level, which is where that statement was intended, it may be true (or have been true), but it is misleading when applied to the motivation of the behaviour of individuals. For most people a moment's reflection indicates that one receives or performs more prosocial acts every day than selfishly assertive ones. Furthermore, it is a matter of common observation that in both pre-industrial and industrial societies individuals co-operate with each other a great deal of the time … I want to emphasize that it is too easy to lose sight of the good side of human nature. Our societies could not exist if prosocial behaviour towards our fellow group members were not the norm. Selfishly assertive behaviour to others is not the norm, though the instances reported by the media are certainly attention-getting. So the first question is, how did these two propensities become part of human social behaviour?

It is easy enough to see how natural selection could induce selfish assertiveness: individuals who looked after their own interests would be more likely to reproduce successfully and would leave more offspring resembling themselves in the next generation. The real problem for biologists has been 'how did the propensity to be prosocial arise?' How could selection produce a tendency to help others who might be competitors for limited resources? Several mechanisms seem likely or possible. First, parental care is found in all mammals: each offspring carries genes from each of its parents, and only if the parent looks after its own young during development will the young survive and pass on the genes in their turn to their offspring. Thus parents enhance the perpetuation of their own genes by looking after their children: by honouring parents children both ensure that they receive parental care and may facilitate their parents' future reproduction. Respect for parents (and ancestors) is found probably in all societies, though the number of generations, and the degree of relatedness for which respect is required, varies. The demands of the young on the parents increase with age, and there comes a point at which the cost to the parent of satisfying the demands of the young exceed the long-term benefits on the parents' lifetime reproductive success: it is then in the parents' interest to wean or reject their offspring.

Beyond that, it will also be of selective value for individuals to behave prosocially to other individuals who are genetically related to them, if the costs they incur in doing so (in terms of the negative effect on their own current and future descendants) are balanced by the positive effects on the reproductive potential of their relatives. The biological value of behaving prosocially to kin will vary with the degree of genetic relatedness: for example, in two-parent families each parent contributes (on average) half of the offspring's genes, one quarter of a grandchild's, one quarter of a nephew's or niece's, one eighth of a cousin's, and so on.

However, this genetic mechanism cannot account for why one should be kind to unrelated individuals. A second mechanism that has been suggested for the genesis of prosociality involves reciprocity: 'I'll do you a good turn if you do one for me.' This is of central importance in maintaining prosociality in human groups, but is unlikely to have been responsible for the evolution of prosociality in large groups.

The third mechanism arises from the fact that our ancestors lived in small groups consisting of one or a few families. These groups would have competed with each other to obtain scarce resources. Competition could involve co-operation within some groups in exploiting the limited resources more efficiently than other groups (for instance co-operation in killing large animals) or physical aggression (perhaps to steal women) directed to competing groups. It is reasonable to assume that members of groups in which the members co-operated with each other would be likely to be more successful than groups whose members were selfishly assertive to each other. Thus selection could promote prosociality towards other group members. Whether competition between groups could result in *genetic* selection for prosociality is controversial, for it is improbable that genetic selection could operate in that way in animals. But, because humans have greater cognitive abilities than any other species, a propensity for co-operation with other group members could be passed on to later generations by several forms of individual learning. It would be advantageous to individuals to belong to a group of appropriately prosocial individuals, and mathematical modelling has shown that, given certain conditions, cultural selection for predominantly prosocial groups could occur …

Changing How We Live: Society from the bottom up by Robert A Hinde, Spokesman, Nottingham, 2011

* * *

Aspects of Chaffinch Behaviour

… Chaffinches are small sexually dimorphic song-birds, common in Western Europe. Marler (1956) studied them in a wood and the surrounding fields near Cambridge. Part of his work involved establishing the basic natural history of the species. During the winter chaffinches feed and roost in flocks, but in early spring the males confine their activities to a particular area, defending it from other males. The fighting is at first centred on certain perches which the males use as song posts. The male's song attracts females. When a female first arrives in a male's territory she may be threatened, but the male soon switches to courtship. After some days or weeks the female starts to build a nest, in which about five eggs are laid. These are incubated by the female, though the male may give some assistance in feeding the young. In late summer the birds undergo a moult, during which they behave very cryptically, before joining the winter flocks.

Ethology: Its nature and relations with other sciences, Robert A Hinde, Fontana Press, Glasgow, 1982

A WINDOW OPEN ON THE WORLD

The UNESCO Courier

SPINA: MYSTERY CITY OF THE ETRUSCANS

THE DIVORCE OF SCIENCE & 'CULTURE'

by
Bertrand Russell

FEBRUARY
1958
(11th year)
Price: 1/-stg. (U. K.)
30 cents (U. S.)
50 francs (France)

The Divorce of Science and 'Culture'

Bertrand Russell

Science cultivates our world in increasingly diverse ways, so that Nottingham UNESCO City of Literature shares a common home with BioCity and life sciences. In 1958, Bertrand Russell urged ending the modern separation of science from culture, when he received the Kalinga Prize for the popularisation of science, at UNESCO House in Paris. His call resonates.

There was a time when scientists looked askance at attempts to make their work widely intelligible. But, in the world of the present day, such an attitude is no longer possible. The discoveries of modern science have put into the hands of governments unprecedented powers both for good and for evil. Unless the statesmen who wield these powers have at least an elementary understanding of their nature, it is scarcely likely that they will use them wisely. And, in democratic countries, it is not only statesmen, but the general public, to whom some degree of scientific understanding is necessary.

To insure wide diffusion of such understanding is by no means easy. Those who can act effectively as liaison officers between technical scientists and the public perform a work which is necessary, not only for human welfare, but even for bare survival of the human race. I think that a great deal more ought to be done in this direction in the education of those who do not intend to become scientific specialists. The Kalinga Prize is doing a great public service in encouraging those who attempt this difficult task.

In my own country, and to a lesser degree in other countries of the West, 'culture' is viewed mainly, by an unfortunate impoverishment of the Renaissance tradition, as something concerned primarily with literature, history and art. A man is not considered uneducated if he knows nothing of the contributions of Galileo, Descartes and their successors. I am convinced that all higher education should involve a course in the history of science from the seventeenth century to the present day and a survey of modern scientific knowledge in so far as this can be conveyed without technicalities. While such knowledge remains confined to specialists, it is scarcely possible nowadays for nations to conduct their affairs with wisdom.

There are two very different ways of estimating any human achievement: you may estimate it by what you consider its intrinsic excellence, or you may estimate it by its causal efficiency in transforming human life and human institutions. I am not suggesting that one of these ways of estimating is preferable to the other. I am only concerned to point out that they give very different scales of importance. If Homer and Aeschylus had not existed, if Dante and Shakespeare had not written a line, if Bach and Beethoven had been silent, the daily life of most people in the present day would have been much what it is. But if Pythagoras and Galileo and James Watt had not existed, the daily life, not only of Western Europeans and Americans but of Indian, Russian and Chinese peasants, would be profoundly different from what it is. And these profound changes are still only beginning. They must affect the future even more than they have already affected the present.

At present, scientific technique advances like an army of tanks that have lost their drivers, blindly, ruthlessly, without goal or purpose. This is largely because the men who are concerned with human values and with making life worthy to be lived, are still living in imagination in the old pre-industrial world, the world that had been made familiar and comfortable by the literature of Greece and the pre-industrial achievements of the poets and artists and composers whose work we rightly admire.

The separation of science from 'culture' is a modern phenomenon. Plato and Aristotle had a profound respect for what was known of science in their day. The Renaissance was as much concerned with the revival of science as with art and literature. Leonardo da Vinci devoted more of his energies to science than to painting. The Renaissance architects developed the geometrical theory of perspective. Throughout the eighteenth century a very great deal was done to diffuse understanding of the work of Newton and his contemporaries. But, from the early nineteenth century onwards, scientific concepts and scientific methods became increasingly abstruse and the attempt to make them generally intelligible came more and more to be regarded as hopeless. The modern theory and practice of nuclear physicists has made evident with dramatic suddenness that complete ignorance of the world of science is no longer compatible with survival.

Pythagoras on a third-century coin

Nottingham and the mining country

D H Lawrence

Nottingham is attempting to develop a long-term 'cultural strategy' for the city region in the English Midlands. How will Nottingham grow locally and at the international level? The Spokesman and the Bertrand Russell Peace Foundation thrive in the Trent Valley, and have done so for almost half a century. Now, faced with profound uncertainties of Brexit, on top of deep-seated effects on the region of precipitate destruction of the coal and much of the textile industries, how might Nottingham cultivate its prospects? To provide some historical perspective, we turn to D H Lawrence who, in 1929, shared singular if sometimes censorious insights about his home patch, the 'intimate community' down pit, and the 'sweep to a civic centre'.

* * *

I was born nearly forty-four years ago, in Eastwood, a mining village of some three thousand souls, about eight miles from Nottingham, and one mile from the small stream, the Erewash, which divides Nottinghamshire from Derbyshire. It is hilly country, looking west to Crich and towards Matlock, sixteen miles away, and east and north-east towards Mansfield and the Sherwood Forest district. To me it seemed, and still seems, an extremely beautiful countryside, just between the red sandstone and the oak-trees of Nottingham, and the cold limestone, the ash-trees, the stone fences of Derbyshire. To me, as a child and a young man, it was still the old England of the forest and agricultural past; there were no motor-cars, the mines were, in a sense, an accident in the landscape, and

Born into a border country mining community in 1885, the celebrated author of Sons and Lovers, The Rainbow *and* Lady Chatterley's Lover *also wrote feisty essays and toe-curling poems, when he hadn't his paintbrush in hand.*

Robin Hood and his merry men were not very far away.

The string of coal-mines of B. W. & Co. had been opened some sixty years before I was born, and Eastwood had come into being as a consequence. It must have been a tiny village at the beginning of the nineteenth century, a small place of cottages and fragmentary rows of little four-roomed miners' dwellings, the homes of the old colliers of the eighteenth century, who worked in the bits of mines, foot-hill mines with an opening in the hillside into which the miners walked, or windlass mines, where the men were wound up one at a time, in a bucket, by a donkey. The windlass mines were still working when my father was a boy – and the shafts of some were still there, when I was a boy.

But somewhere about 1820 the company must have sunk the first big shaft – not very deep – and installed the first machinery of the real industrial colliery. Then came my grandfather, a young man trained to be a tailor, drifting from the south of England, and got the job of company tailor for the Brinsley mine. In those days the company supplied the men with the thick flannel vests, or singlets, and the moleskin trousers lined at the top with flannel, in which the colliers worked. I remember the great rolls of course flannel and pit-cloth which stood in the corner of my grandfather's shop when I was a small boy, and the big, strange old sewing-machine, like nothing else on earth, which sewed the massive pit-trousers. But when I was only a child the company discontinued supplying the men with pit-clothes.

My grandfather settled in an old cottage down in a quarry-bed, by the brook at Old Brinsley, near the pit. A mile away, up at Eastwood, the company built the first miners' dwellings – it must be nearly a hundred years ago. Now Eastwood occupies a lovely position on a hilltop, with the steep slope towards Derbyshire and the long slope towards Nottingham. They put up a new church, which stands fine and commanding, even if it has no real form, looking across the awful Erewash Valley at the church of Heanor, similarly commanding, away on a hill beyond. What opportunities, what opportunities! These mining villages *might* have been like the lovely hill-towns of Italy, shapely and fascinating. And what happened?

Most of the little rows of dwellings of the old-style miners were pulled down, and dull little shops began to rise along the Nottingham Road, while on the down-slope of the north side the company erected what is still known as the New Buildings, or the Square. These New Buildings consist of two great hollow squares of dwellings planked down on the rough slope of the hill, little four-room houses with the 'front' looking outward into the grim, blank street, and the 'back', with a tiny square brick yard, a low wall, and a w.c. and ash-pit, looking into the desert of the square, hard, uneven, jolting black earth tilting rather steeply down, with these little back yards all round, and openings at the corners. The squares were quite big, and absolutely desert, save for the posts for clothes lines, and people passing, children playing on the hard earth. And they were shut in like a barracks enclosure, very strange.

Even fifty years ago the squares were unpopular. It was 'common' to live in the Square. It was a little less common to live in the Breach, which consisted of six blocks of rather more pretentious dwellings erected by the company in the valley below, two rows of three blocks, with an alley between. And it was most 'common', most degraded of all to live in Dakins Row, two rows of the old dwellings, very old, black four-roomed little places, that stood on the hill again, not far from the Square.

So the place started. Down the steep street between the squares, Scargill Street, the Wesleyans' chapel was put up, and I was born in the little corner shop just above. Across the other side of the Square the miners themselves built the big, barn-like Primitive Methodist chapel. Along the hill-top ran the Nottingham Road, with its scrappy, ugly mid-Victorian shops. The little market-place, with a superb outlook, ended the village on the Derbyshire side, and was just here left bare, with the Sun Inn on one side, the chemist across, with the gilt pestle-and-mortar, and a shop at the other corner, the corner of Alfreton Road and Nottingham Road.

In this queer jumble of the old England and the new, I came into consciousness. As I remember, little local speculators already began to straggle dwellings in rows, always in rows, across the fields: nasty red-brick, flat-faced dwellings with dark slate roofs. The bay-window period only began when I was a child. But most of the country was untouched.

There must be three or four hundred company houses in the squares and the streets that surround the squares, like a great barracks wall. There must be sixty or eighty company houses in the Breach. The old Dakins Row will have thirty to forty little holes. Then counting the old cottages and rows left with their old gardens down the lanes and along the twitchells, and even in the midst of Nottingham Road itself, there were houses enough for the population, there was no need for much building. And not much building went on when I was small.

We lived in the Breach, in a corner house. A field-path came down under a great hawthorn hedge. On the other side was the brook, with the old sheep-bridge going over into the meadows. The hawthorn hedge by the brook had grown tall as tall trees, and we used to bathe from there in the dipping-hole, where the sheep were dipped, just near the fall from the old mill-dam, where the water rushed. The mill only ceased grinding the local corn when I was a child. And my father, who always worked in Brinsley pit, and who always got up at five o'clock, if not at four, would set off in the dawn across the fields at Coney Grey, and hunt for mushrooms in the long grass, or perhaps pick up a skulking rabbit, which he would bring home at evening inside the lining of his pit-coat.

So that the life was a curious cross between industrialism and the old agricultural England of Shakespeare and Milton and Fielding and George Eliot. The dialect was broad Derbyshire, and always 'thee' and 'thou'. The people lived almost entirely by instinct, men of my father's age could not really read. And the pit did not mechanize men. On the contrary. Under the butty system, the miners worked underground as a sort of intimate community, they knew each other practically naked, and with curious close intimacy, and the darkness and the underground remoteness of the pit 'stall', and the continual presence of danger, made the physical, instinctive, and intuitional contact between men very highly developed, a contact almost as close as touch, very real and very powerful. This physical awareness and intimate *togetherness* was at its strongest down pit. When the men came up into the light, they blinked. They had, in a measure, to change their flow. Nevertheless, they brought with them above ground the curious dark intimacy of the mine, the naked sort of contact, and if I think of my childhood, it is always as if there was a lustrous sort of inner darkness, like the gloss of coal, in which we moved and had our real being. My father loved the pit. He was hurt badly, more than once, but he would never stay away. He loved the contact, the intimacy, as men in the war loved the intense male comradeship of the dark days. They did not know what they had till they lost it. And I think it is the same with the young colliers of today.

Now the colliers had also an instinct of beauty. The colliers' wives had not. The colliers were deeply alive, instinctively. But they had no daytime ambition, and no daytime intellect. They avoided, really, the rational aspect of life. They preferred to take life instinctively and intuitively. They didn't even care very profoundly about wages. It was the women, naturally, who nagged on this score. There was a big discrepancy, when I was a boy, between the collier who saw, at the best, only a brief few hours of daylight – often no daylight at all during the winter weeks – and the collier's wife, who had all the day to herself when the man was down pit.

The great fallacy is, to pity the man. He didn't dream of pitying himself, till agitators and sentimentalists taught him to. He was happy: or more than happy, he was fulfilled. Or he was fulfilled on the receptive side, not on the expressive. The collier went to the pub and drank in order to continue his intimacy with his mates. They talked endlessly, but it was rather of wonders and marvels, even in politics, than of facts. It was hard facts, in the shape of wife, money, and nagging home necessities, which they fled away from, out of the house to the pub, and out of the house to the pit.

The collier fled out of the house as soon as he could, away from the nagging materialism of the woman. With the women it was always: this is broken, now you've got to mend it! Or else: we want this, that, and the other, and where is the money coming from? The collier didn't know and didn't care very deeply – his life was otherwise. So he escaped. He roved the countryside with his dog, prowling for a rabbit, for nests, for mushrooms, anything. He loved the countryside, just the indiscriminating feel of it. Or he loved just to sit on his heels and watch – anything of nothing. He was not intellectually interested. Life for him did not consist in facts, but in a flow. Very often, he loved his garden. And very often he had a genuine love of the beauty of flowers. I have known it often and often, in colliers.

Now the love of flowers is a very misleading thing. Most women love flowers as possessions, and as trimmings. They can't look at a flower, and wonder a moment, and pass on. If they see a flower that arrests their attention, they must at once pick it, pluck it. Possession! A possession! Something added on to *me!* And most of the so-called love of flowers today is merely this reaching out of possession and egoism: something I've *got*: something that embellishes *me*. Yet I've seen many a collier stand in his back garden looking down at a flower with that odd, remote sort of contemplation which shows a *real* awareness of the presence of beauty. It would not even be admiration, or joy, or delight, or any of those things which so often have a root in the possessive instinct. It would be a sort of contemplation: which shows an incipient artist.

The real tragedy of England, as I see it, is the tragedy of ugliness. The country is so lovely: the man-made England is so vile. I know that the ordinary collier, when I was a boy, had a peculiar sense of beauty, coming from his intuitive and instinctive consciousness, which was awakened down pit. And the fact that he met with just cold ugliness and raw materialism when he came up into daylight, and particularly when he came to the Square or the Breach, and to his own table, killed something in him, and in a sense spoiled him as a man. The woman almost invariably nagged about material things. She was taught to do it; she was encouraged to do it. It was a mother's business to see that her sons 'got on', and it was the man's business to provide the money. In my father's generation, with the old wild England behind them, and the lack of education, the man was not beaten down. But in my generation, the boys I went to school with, colliers now, have all been beaten down, what with the din-din-dinning of Board Schools, cinemas, clergymen, the whole national and human consciousness hammering on the fact of material prosperity above all things.

The men are beaten down, there is prosperity for a time, in their defeat – and then disaster looms ahead. The root of all disaster is disheartenment. And men are disheartened. The men of England, the colliers in particular, are disheartened. They have been betrayed and beaten.

Now though perhaps nobody knew it, it was ugliness which betrayed the spirit of man, in the nineteenth century. The great crime which the moneyed classes and promoters of industry committed in the palmy Victorian days was the condemning of the workers to ugliness, ugliness, ugliness: meanness and formless and ugly surroundings, ugly ideals, ugly religion, ugly hope, ugly love, ugly clothes, ugly furniture, ugly houses, ugly relationship between workers and employers. The human soul needs actual beauty even more than bread. The middle classes jeer at the colliers for buying pianos – but what is the piano, often as not, but a blind reaching out for beauty? To the woman it is a possession and a piece of furniture and something to feel superior about. But see the elderly colliers trying to learn to play, see them listening with queer alert faces to their daughter's execution of *The Maiden's Prayer*, and you will see a blind, unsatisfied craving for beauty. It is far more deep in the men than in the women. The women want show. The men want beauty, and still want it.

If the company, instead of building those sordid and hideous Squares, then, when they had that lovely site to play with, there on the hill top: if they had put a tall column in the middle of the small market-place, and run three parts of a circle of arcade round the pleasant space, where people could stroll or sit, and with the handsome houses behind! If they had made big, substantial houses, in apartments of five and six rooms, and with handsome entrances. If above all, they had encouraged song and dancing – for the miners still sang and danced – and provided handsome space for these. If only they had encouraged some form of beauty in dress, some form of beauty in interior life – furniture, decoration. If they had given prizes for the handsomest chair or table, the loveliest scarf, the most charming room that the men or women could make! If only they had done this, there would never have been an industrial problem. The industrial problem arises from the base forcing of all human energy into a competition of mere acquisition.

You may say the working man would not have accepted such a form of life: the Englishman's home is his castle, etc., etc. – 'my own little home'. But if you can hear every word the next-door-people say, there's not much castle. And if you can see everybody in the square if they go to the w.c.! And if your one desire is to get out of the 'castle' and your 'own little home'! – well, there's not much to be said for it. Anyhow it's only the woman who idolizes 'her own little home' – and it's always the woman at her worst, her most greedy, most possessive, most mean. There's nothing to be said for the 'little home' any more: a great scrabble of ugly pettiness over the face of the land.

As a matter of fact, till 1800 the English people were strictly a rural people – very rural. England has had towns for centuries, but they have never been real towns, only clusters of village streets. Never the real *urbs*. The English character has failed to develop the real *urban* side of a man, the civic side. Siena is a bit of a place, but it is a real city, with citizens intimately connected with the city. Nottingham is a vast place sprawling towards a million, and it is nothing more than an amorphous agglomeration. There *is* no Nottingham, in the sense that there is Siena. The Englishman is stupidly undeveloped, as a citizen. And it is partly due to his 'little home' stunt, and partly to his acceptance of hopeless paltriness in his surrounding. The new cities of America are much more genuine cities, in the Roman sense, than is London or Manchester. Even Edinburgh used to be more of a true city than any town England ever produced.

That silly little individualism of 'the Englishman's home is his castle' and 'my own little home' is out of date. It would work almost up to 1800, when every Englishman was still a villager, and a cottager. But the industrial system has brought a great change. The Englishman still likes to think of himself as a 'cottager' – 'my home, my garden'. But it is puerile. Even the farm labourer today is psychologically a town-bird. The English are town-birds through and through, today, as the inevitable result of their complete industrialization. Yet they don't know how to build a city, how to think of one, or how to live in one. They are all suburban, pseudo-cottagy, and not one of them knows how to be truly urban – the citizens as the Romans were citizens – or the Athenians – or even the Parisians, till the war came.

And this is because we have frustrated that instinct of community which would make us unite in pride and dignity in the bigger gesture of the citizen, not the cottager. The great city means beauty, dignity, and a certain splendour. This is the side of the Englishman that has been thwarted and shockingly betrayed. England is a mean and petty scrabble of paltry dwellings called 'homes'. I believe in their heart of hearts all Englishmen loathe their little homes – but not the women. What we want is a bigger gesture, a greater scope, a certain splendour, a certain grandeur, and beauty, big beauty. The American does far better than we, in this.

And the promoter of industry, a hundred years ago, dared to perpetrate the ugliness of my native village. And still more monstrous, promoters of industry today are scrabbling over the face of England with miles and square miles of red-brick 'homes', like horrible scabs. And the men inside these little red rat-traps get more and more helpless, being more and more humiliated, more and more dissatisfied, like trapped rats. Only the meaner sort of women go on loving the little home which is no more than a rat-trap to her man.

Do away with it all, then. At no matter what cost, start in to alter it. Never mind about wages and industrial squabbling. Turn the attention elsewhere. Pull down my native village to the last brick. Plan a nucleus. Fix the focus. Make a handsome gesture of radiation from the focus. And then put up big buildings, handsome, that sweep to a civic centre. And furnish them with beauty. And make an absolute clean start. Do it place by place. Make a new England. Away with little homes! Away with scrabbling pettiness and paltriness. Look at the contours of the land, and build up from these, with a sufficient nobility. The English may be mentally or spiritually developed. But as citizens of splendid cities they are more ignominious than rabbits. And they nag, nag, nag all the time about politics and wages and all that, like mean narrow housewives.

Written in 1929, this essay was published in The New Adelphi*, June-August, 1930, and* Phoenix*, 1936.*

UNESCO

NOTTINGHAM
City of Literature

United Nations
Educational, Scientific and
Cultural Organization

Designated
UNESCO Creative City
in 2015

SNAKE

A snake came to my water-trough
On a hot, hot day, and I in pyjamas for the heat,
To drink there.

In the deep, strange-scented shade of the great dark carob-tree
I came down the steps with my pitcher
And must wait, must stand and wait, for there he was at the trough before me.

He reached down from a fissure in the earth-wall in the gloom
And trailed his yellow-brown slackness soft-bellied down, over the edge of the stone trough
And rested his throat upon the stone bottom,
And where the water had dripped from the tap, in a small clearness,
He sipped with his straight mouth,
Softly drank through his straight gums, into his slack long body,
Silently.

Someone was before me at my water-trough,
And I, like a second comer, waiting.

He lifted his head from his drinking, as cattle do,
And looked at me vaguely, as drinking cattle do,
And flickered his two-forked tongue from his lips, and mused a moment,
And stooped and drank a little more,
Being earth-brown, earth-golden from the burning bowels of the earth
On the day of Sicilian July, with Etna smoking.

The voice of my education said to me
He must be killed,
For in Sicily the black, black snakes are innocent, the gold are venomous.

And voices in me said, If you were a man
You would take a stick and break him now, and finish him off.

But must I confess how I liked him,
How glad I was he had come like a guest in quiet, to drink at my water-trough
And depart peaceful, pacified, and thankless,
Into the burning bowels of this earth?

Was it cowardice, that I dared not kill him?
Was it perversity, that I longed to talk to him?
Was it humility, to feel so honoured?
I felt so honoured.
And yet those voices:
If you were not afraid, you would kill him!

And truly I was afraid, I was most afraid,
But even so, honoured still more
That he should seek my hospitality
From out the dark door of the secret earth.

He drank enough
And lifted his head, dreamily, as one who has drunken,
And flickered his tongue like a forked night on the air, so black,
Seeming to lick his lips,
And looked around like a god, unseeing, into the air,
And slowly turned his head,
And slowly, very slowly, as if thrice adream,
Proceeded to draw his slow length curving round
And climb again the broken bank of my wall-face.

And as he put his head into that dreadful hole,
And as he slowly drew up, snake-easing his shoulders, and entered farther,
A sort of horror, a sort of protest against his withdrawing into that horrid black hole,
Deliberately going into the blackness, and slowly drawing himself after,
Overcame me now his back was turned.

I looked round, I put down my pitcher,
I picked up a clumsy log
And threw it at the water-trough with a clatter.

I think it did not hit him,
But suddenly that part of him that was left behind convulsed in undignified haste,
Writhed like lightning, and was gone
Into the black hole, the earth-lipped fissure in the wall-front,
At which, in the intense still noon, I stared with fascination.

And immediately I regretted it.
I thought how paltry, how vulgar, what a mean act!
I despised myself and the voices of my accursed human education.

And I thought of the albatross
And I wished he would come back, my snake.

For he seemed to me again like a king,
Like a king in exile, uncrowned in the underworld,
Now due to be crowned again.

And so, I missed my chance with one of the lords
Of life.
And I have something to expiate:
A pettiness.

David Herbert Lawrence
Taormina, 1923

Dawn of the UNREAD
MAD MADGE
-FEATURING-
ROLLER GRRRLS
-AND-
MARGARET CAVENDISH
NOTTINGHAM
WRITERS
STUDI
GARY ERSKINE
ARTIST
MHAIRI STEWART
WRITER
JAMES WALKER
DIRECTOR/EDITOR
PAUL FILLINGHAM
ART/DIGITAL PRODUCER
LOTTERY FUNDED
Supported using public funding by
ARTS COUNCIL ENGLAND
DAWN OF THE UNREAD - BASED ON AN IDEA BY JAMES WALKER

Reviews

Decent intellect?

George Orwell, Peter Davison (editor), *Seeing Things As They Are: Selected journalism and other writings*, Harvill Secker, 2014, 484 pages, hardback ISBN 1846558993, £25

Still going strong at 90, Peter Davison (*not* the Dr Who homonym) is the doyen of Orwell studies.

After kicking off with *George Orwell: A Literary Life* (1996), he (with Sheila Davison and Ian Angus) put the world in debt with 20 volumes of *The Complete Works of George Orwell* (1998), thus amplifying, indeed superseding, the previous front-runner, a 4-volume *Collected Essays, Journalism & Letters of George Orwell* (1968) by Ian Angus and Sonia Orwell (his widow), now out of print. Since then, Davison has further blessed us with *The Lost Orwell* (2007), *George Orwell: A Life in Letters* (2011), and an edition of Orwell's *Diaries* (2013).

The best way to keep up with the unabated flood of Orwelliana – itself a tribute to Davison as a tributary – is via the Orwell Society, launched in 2011, details via its website.

Apropos of Sonia (née Brownell), Orwell met her when she worked on Cyril Connolly's *Horizon*, the magazine that was the glue for London's literary life during the Second World War. According to such friends as Anthony Powell, she was great comfort to Orwell in his last months. There was, inevitably, a suggestion (from the late Jenny Diski) that she married him for his fame and growing fortune. Over the years, including a disastrous second marriage to Michael Pitt-Rivers, she developed drinking problems, saw herself as the keeper of George's flame, and was prickly towards aspirant biographers.

This raises a permanently tricky point. Orwell's will stipulated that there be no biography. Other luminaries (A. E. Housman, for example) did the same. Their wishes have not been respected. Should they have been? In principle, I say *yes*, but as Groucho Marx said, 'if you don't like my principles, I have others,' and I eagerly read every Life of Orwell that comes out.

As hinted in the titular *Girl from the Fiction Department*, Hilary Spurling's well-balanced biography (2002), Sonia was the model for Julia in *1984*. There may also have been echoes of Orwell's first wife, Eileen O'Shaugnessy, who back in 1934 had written for her school magazine a poem 'End of the Century 1984'; whatever the precise truth, a complementary model. Julia (I am listening to the Eurythmics' eponymous ballad as I write) is frequently far more percipient than Winston; on this, and for full consideration of the strengths and weaknesses of the novel, see my essay available on the websites ReadySteadyBook and Shattercolors. Whilst *1984* plays no big part in this Davison volume, he does reproduce a Winston-Julia scene from Orwell's manuscript, omitted (rightly) in the published version.

Davison includes a wide range of Orwell's articles, essays, film and theatre reviews, BBC broadcasts, and a lavish selection of his 'As I Please' pieces from *Tribune*. One might question the point of this last, given that the entire collection was published with valuable annotations by Paul Anderson in 2006. Since they are my favourites, I don't really mind, though they occupy space that might have been used for (e.g.) his (Samuel Johnson-inspired?) piece, 'A Nice Cup of Tea' (*Evening Standard*, 12 January 1946).

A number of pieces settle once and for all long-dragged-out debates over the sources and purpose of *1984*. Orwell publicly stated, 'my novel is not an attack on socialism, or on the British Labour Party (of which I am a supporter). It is a satire …' His discussion of James Burnham's notion (*Managerial Revolution*) of a world divided between two or three superstates permanently at (real or imaginary?) war, and his review of Zamyatin's novel *We,* both published in 1946, are conclusive inspirational evidence.

Davison includes a few previously unpublished items: a BBC discussion of *Wigan Pier*; a letter to Victor Gollancz about *Animal Farm*; an article withdrawn from *Tribune* on the trials of Poles in Moscow – a piece on Polish immigration to Britain could have been written yesterday; Daniel George's pioneering BBC critique of Orwell as an essayist.

Of special interest to *Spokesman* readers will be Orwell's review of Bertrand Russell's *Power: A New Social Analysis*, published in *The Adelphi*, January 1939, concluding 'this book, though it is not so good as *Freedom and Organisation,* is very well worth reading'. Russell would be a great, public admirer of *1984*. Orwell characteristically combines lavish praise with epigrammatic digs, as these extracts show:

> 'Like all liberals, he is better at pointing out what is desirable than at explaining how to achieve it … Mr Russell is one of the most readable of living writers, and it is very reassuring to know that he exists. So long as he and a few others like him are alive and out of jail, we know that the world is still sane in parts. He has rather an eclectic mind, he is capable of saying shallow things and profoundly interesting things in alternate sentences … He has an essentially

> *decent* intellect, a kind of intellectual chivalry which is far rarer than mere cleverness. Few people during the last thirty years have been so consistently impervious to the fashionable bunk of the moment.'

Near the end of his life, though, Orwell was markedly less kind. Along with (rightly) putting the boot into Sartre's *Portrait of an Antisemite* – a topic on which he himself frequently appears in Davison's assemblage – he said of Russell's *Human Knowledge: Its Scope and Limits* that it made him feel philosophy should be made illegal.

Overall, it is hard to see how Davison or anyone else can go to this anthological well one more time. Unless, that is, there are significant new discoveries, most likely – I would guess – to surface in the BBC wartime archives and/or letters in private hands. But, Orwell (and Samuel Johnson – the two had more in common than you might suppose, apart from tea) are my heroes, hence I never tire of re-reading whatever each anthologiser chooses to throw up.

Barry Baldwin

Civilisation or enslavement?

Mary Beard, *SPQR – A history of ancient Rome*, Profile Books, 2015, 606 pages, ISBN 9781846683800, £25

A thousand years of Roman history, from the myths surrounding Romulus and Remus to the granting of Roman citizenship to all free men and women by the Emperor Caracalla in 212 CE, is the subject of Mary Beard's *SPQR*. The Senate and People of Rome (Senatus Populusque Romanus) or SPQR was a 'shorthand slogan' for the legitimate power of the Roman state and is a term that still resonates in Italy today. This book focuses on the early settlement and growth of ancient Rome and its Empire, concentrating not just on the internal politics of a myriad of senators and emperors (and the Roman elite more generally) but also the changing relationships between an ever-expanding Rome and its various neighbours. But this is not a simple history of the powerful men who made Rome and the successes (and occasional failures) of Roman legions across the known world. What Mary Beard has succeeded in creating is a riveting, extended discussion of how Roman political institutions were moulded by territorial and population growth on an unprecedented scale. How does she do this? Firstly, Mary Beard is someone who is at the very top of her game.

She has spent 50 years as a classicist studying texts (ancient and modern), digging up ruins, exploring sites across Europe and Africa, and reading monuments and tomb epitaphs. Secondly, she is an excellent communicator: writing a clear and captivating story. Latin, a supposedly dead language, comes alive on these pages! Thirdly, she is able to engage with an exceptional range of sources to illustrate her points and broaden her discussion: original documents, inscriptions, poems, paintings, letters and speeches. The book is also packed with black and white and full colour photographs of buildings, wall paintings, maps, tombs, sculpture, jewellery and miscellaneous, unexpected items (like a slave's neck-ring with instructions on where to send the slave if they escaped).

SPQR is a popular history of Rome for the general reader (even though it is over 600 pages long) but it is not simply a work of 'admiration'. As Beard points out, while there is a lot 'to engage our interest and demand our attention', there is also a lot which is baffling or completely unacceptable to us now: child brides, abandoning unwanted babies on rubbish dumps, slavery, the slaughter in the arena and, surprisingly, the filth (for example, Rome, a city of millions by the time of the Empire, had no rubbish collection).

Mary Beard also has the ability to draw the reader into discussions which are as relevant now as they were when they first occurred in Roman history, despite widely differing circumstances: the role of the state and its limits, political and personal morality, the perils of myth-making (for emperors and historians), and the realities of military conquest, then and now. For example, the conquest of Gaul by Julius Caesar was likened to genocide by some contemporary writers, and Britain had a similar fate, though this is now often overlooked. And she encourages us to think. Some 'history' is likely to be myth – for example, Cleopatra's snakebite suicide in 32BCE. As Beard comments, 'suicide by snake bite is a hard feat to pull off, and anyway, the most reliably deadly snakes would be far too hefty to conceal in even a regal fruit bowl'. It is more likely that she was done away with, whether by her compatriots or her captors we will never know.

SPQR can be divided into two halves. The first part concentrates on the founding of Rome, its steady growth under a series of kings (or chiefs), and the ways in which the Roman Republic was governed with two annually elected Consuls and a Senate. The second part starts with the autocratic rule of the first emperor Augustus, the different emperors who followed him, and the increasing irrelevance of the Senate. Mary Beard makes the point that it is necessary to 'squeeze' as much out of remaining artefacts as possible to construct a picture of early Rome but, by the time of Augustus, the problem is the exact opposite, with selection from an abundance of evidence being necessary.

This abundance enables her to draw a picture of what life might have been like for Roman citizens and others, not just at the centre of the Empire but far away from Rome, living in a province under a governor. For example, Pliny, (the Roman governor of Bithynia, appointed in 109 CE) wrote regularly to the Emperor Trajan requesting decisions about local issues in the province. Bithynia was on the southern shore of the Black Sea and at least four weeks travel (and nearly two thousand miles) away from Rome. One of his problems was that of Christianity, 'a perverse and unruly superstition', and what to do about stubborn Christians who refused to give up their faith.

And Beard is able to identify the other ways in which the power of the Roman Empire was consolidated over such a wide area: through the army's role in administration, through the collaboration of significant locals, and through cultural incorporation. She is able to use the historian Tacitus' accounts of the achievements of Agricola, governor of Britain from 77 to 85CE, to show this in detail. Agricola, we are told, organised a programme of education for the sons of the local elite – in the 'liberal arts' and Latin. Soon they were dressing in togas, using the Roman public baths and adopting other Roman habits – such that he could remark, 'they call it, in their ignorance, "civilisation" but it was really part of their enslavement'.

SPQR ends with Caracalla's grant of citizenship across the Empire to any free man or woman. No one knows why he did it, but at a stroke he removed the distinction between rulers and ruled. But there was to be no happy ending. New divisions emerged in the third century BCE between the *honestiores* ('the most honourable') or rich elite and the *humiliores* ('the lower sort'), with unequal rights written into Roman law. But more significantly, by the third century BCE, the Empire was torn apart by extended civil war as rivals for the position of Emperor often sought power with the help of the army. The ways in which power was distributed across the Empire in the centuries that followed changed dramatically.

Beard comments that what we may learn from the Romans is not how to conquer or how to rule but rather the extent to which the western world has been influenced by Rome and its Empire: '… many of our most fundamental assumptions about power, citizenship, responsibility, political violence, empire, luxury and beauty have been formed, and tested, in dialogue with the Romans and their writing'. And it may be added, this is a continuous dialogue which continues to produce surprises. Until recently, we knew nothing of the black Africans guarding Hadrian's Wall in Cumbria, the high status black Roman families living in York in the second century CE, and the oldest black Britain, a sub-Saharan African woman living a peaceable life near Beachy Head in Sussex in the first century CE. Some parts of Britain were, it seems, more multi-cultural in Roman times than they are in the twenty-first century. Now what does that tell us about migration, settlement and the British character?

Cathy Davis

Light shining in London

John Rees, *The Leveller Revolution: Radical Political Organisation in England, 1640-1650*, Verso, 2016, 512 pages, hardback ISBN 9781784783884, £25, eISBN 9781784783914, £15

'To our generation fell the good fortune of re-discovering the Levellers,' wrote H N Brailsford in his preface to *The Levellers and the English Revolution*, edited and prepared for publication by Christopher Hill. Brailsford died in 1958, leaving his incomplete yet large manuscript bereft of Introduction and Conclusion. According to Hill, Brailsford thought of his book not as 'a mere history', but as a 'profoundly political study' conveying a message from him to the younger generation. In Brailsford's assessment, one of the main achievements of his book was to prove that, at decisive moments in the seventeenth-century English Revolution, 'the intellectual and political initiative lay with the Levellers, and that Cromwell and the Independent Grandees followed their lead'.

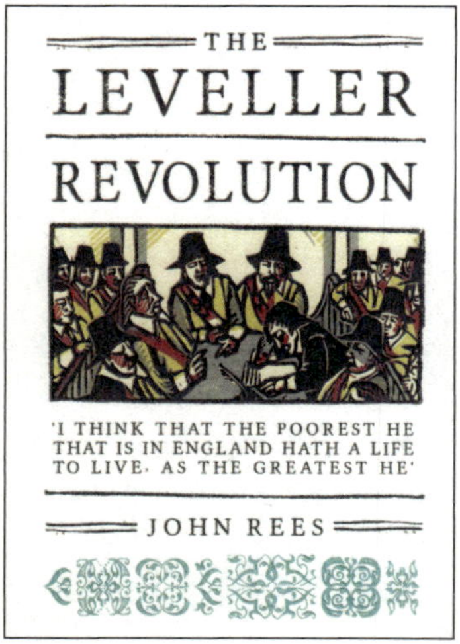

So it is, some 60 years later, that John Rees has taken up the baton passed by Brailsford via Hill and others, and presented the Levellers to a new generation of activists. He has written, as he says in his Introduction, 'primarily a political history' focusing on the 'construction of Leveller organisation', which tends to confirm Brailsford's assessment that, for a tumultuous period in English history, the political initiative lay with the Levellers. The printing press, tavern and ale house figure centrally in Rees' discourse, as much as the diversity of churches and religious gatherings which flowed from the Reformation, the religious revolution of the previous century which gave rise to various evangelical and Protestant organisations of Christendom.

'London was the incubator and mainstay of the Leveller movement,' according to Rees. And he goes on to give a thrilling account of the goings-on in the walled City of London, with its companies of skilled trades. John Lilburne, 'Freeborn John', bright star of the Levellers movement, was apprenticed to a cloth merchant at Londonstone, now Cannon Street. Like so many others, Lilburne had travelled to the capital from his native North-East, aged 14 years, to learn his trade. Another migrant was Katherine Chidley, who became a close comrade of Lilburne. She travelled with her large family from Shrewsbury in 1629, fleeing religious persecution. Such migrations established personal links to the capital across England. In December 1637, Lilburne was arrested, the first of many occasions, for distributing pamphlets by the Puritan martyrs, Henry Burton, John Bastwick, and William Prynne, who had had their ears severed whilst pilloried, and their books burned before their eyes. Members of the Stationers' Company, which controlled 'legal' printing, seized Lilburne.

A mile or so up river, in Westminster, life was also eventful, in keeping with the times. In January 1648, as the English Revolution roared on, Lilburne and fellow Leveller John Wildman were accused of traitorous conspiracy in promoting *The Earnest Petition of many Free-born People of this Nation,* concerning those in Parliament's camp who would compromise with the King. Lilburne and Wildman defended themselves at length at the bar of the House of Commons, but were eventually arrested after swords were drawn. Rees tells us that 'Lilburne thought that one sally would have "undoubtedly dispatched me" had not Elizabeth Lilburne "stood betwixt me and them".' Rees continues his forensic examination of Leveller discussions as he probes their organisation at this critical juncture. A year later, in January 1649, Charles I would lose his head on the scaffold in Whitehall, Colonel Hacker presiding. Seven months after that, in August 1649, Lilburne published yet another pamphlet, *An Impeachment for High Treason against Oliver Cromwell and his son in law Henry Ireton Esquires*, incorporating his earlier speech at the bar of the Commons. Clearly, Lilburne was willing to challenge the mightiest in the land. Rees reckons such petitioning, pamphleteering and related activities 'speaks of a widespread and relatively cohesive organisation' amongst the Levellers, 'with leaders capable of coordinating both their own efforts and those of their supporters', of which there were many throughout England.

For it was certainly the case that much of the decisive action during the 1640s took place far from the capital. Nottingham, for example, was where Charles I raised his standard at the commencement of the Civil War, in 1642. This was not without problems, as Robert Thoroton and John Throsby recount:

> 'The King came to *Nottingham* July the 10th following, and there promised to act according to the protestation at *York*; and in August 22 he erected his standard at *Nottingham*.
>
> 'Nalson in his trial of King CHARLES I mentions the evidence of one Samuel Lawson, of *Nottingham*, maltster, who deposed that about August 1642, he saw the King's standard brought forth of *Nottingham* castle … the standard was first erected on the highest turret of the old tower, (which THOROTON attests as his own remembrance, to have been the 22nd of August, in the castle,) but that after a few days, people not resorting to it according to expectation, it was judged that upon the account of the castle being a garrison, where every body had not so free access to the standard as if it was erected in an open place, it might be proper to remove it out of the castle, which was accordingly done on 25 August, into the close adjoining to the north side of the wall of the outer-ward of the castle, then called the Hill close, and afterwards for many years Standard-Close.'
>
> *The Antiquities of Nottinghamshire, p54*

Apparently, moving the King's standard outside the walls of Nottingham Castle did not address Charles's fundamental problem, which was that he was already deeply unpopular. From 1629 to 1640, he had chosen to reign without Parliament, thus heightening acute political tensions in seventeenth century England. Charles alienated many of his 'subjects' by demanding money through Crown privilege and other devices. So comparatively few rallied to the flag, whether inside the walls of Nottingham Castle or out. The auguries were bad, as Thoroton and Throsby record:

> 'One remarkable accident happened at the first setting up of this standard in the just mentioned close, viz. That the weather grew so tempestuous that it was blown down soon after it was erected, and could not be fixed again in a day or two. This … was looked upon by many melancholy people as a fatal presage of the war.'

Fatal it eventually proved for Charles, and for many of his subjects. Meanwhile, the Levellers' drive for democratic and social reform gave political direction during the formative years of the Interregnum. 'They would have won for our peasants in the mid-17th century what the Great Revolution gained for those of France at the close of the 18th century', in Brailsford's assessment. John Rees' handsome and readable volume elucidates how that world was turned upside down.

Tony Simpson

The Levellers and the English Revolution, *by H N Brailsford, edited by Christopher Hill, published by Spokesman (Socialist Classics 5), £18.*

Day of the Sardine

Sid Chaplin & Michael Chaplin (ed.), *HAME: My Durham*, Mayfly Press, 2016, 320 pages, paperback ISBN 9781911356059, £12.99

If you're not up on Geordie-Speak, 'Hame' is here defined as 'Home' (from Scandinavian/Old Norse).

As Alan Sillitoe rallied Raleigh, so Sid Chaplin was a major miner; the latter was to Newcastle as the former to Nottingham. This rich Centenary collection of essays, fictions, and poems, plus the planned re-printings, will reverse Chaplin's neglect (albeit Google discloses 427,000 websites). The writer D.J.Taylor frequently complains about this, notably Chaplin's virtual omission from Margaret Drabble's *Oxford Companion to English Literature* (1985, 2000) in her minimalist section on 'Regional Novel', dismissing Chaplin as derivative from Lewis Grassic Gibbon's *A Scots Quair* – typical Hampstead snobbery.

Immediate applause for the physical pleasure afforded by the luxurious, indeed sensuous, paper on which *HAME* is printed. I doubt this Tyne & Wear-based press is flush with money, but it has pulled out all the stops here – a rebuking contrast to the many shoddy productions from elsewhere.

For supplements to both *HAME* and review, see: D. J. Taylor's two articles (*TLS* 26 October 2016; *Guardian* 29 April 2016); University of Newcastle website for inventoried Chaplin papers; YouTube for Alan Plater's 1968 musical version of 'Close the Coal-house Door', animated version of 'The Pigeon Cree', and Peter Flannery's 1996 drama series 'Our Friends in the North', showing clear signs of influence by *The Day of the Sardine.*

Contrariwise, Chaplin's break-through *Sardine* (1961) has obvious echoes of Sillitoe's *Saturday Night and Sunday Morning* (1958), e.g. both protagonists are called Arthur, both have affairs with neglected wives. Taylor scintillatingly links the pair:

> 'The world inhabited by Arthur Haggerston and his ever-anxious mother is spiritually only a trolley-bus ride away from the Nottingham tenement graced by Sillitoe's Arthur: a kind of anarchic backwater where authority is held in stony contempt.'

Just as Sillitoe was not an isolated figure in Nottingham working-class literature (details in my review of his celebratory *More Raw Material*, at *Spokesman 132*, p87-89), so Chaplin was part of a Newcastle tradition, notably Harry Hislop's *Last Cage Down* (1936) and Jack Common's multifarious Tyneside tomes, notably *Seven Shifts* (1936) and *Kiddar's Luck* (1951). In more general terms, Taylor sees Chaplin as 'the fictional equivalent' to Hoggart's seminal *The Uses of Literacy* (1957), also adducing such familiar names as Stan Barstow (miner's son) and early John Braine (briefly a factory worker).

Common and Chaplin had one other thing in common: friendship with Orwell (whose wife Eileen, coincidentally, died in a Newcastle hospital). Chaplin asked small shopkeeper Common (as he became) for advice in setting up his own Wallington one, praising the essays in his *The Freedom of the Streets* (1938) as 'the authentic voice of the working man'.

According to Chaplin's widow, Rene, in 1943-44, apart from publishing his literary essays (e.g. on Wilfred Owen) in *Tribune*, Orwell asked Chaplin to fill in on his famous (and my Orwellian desert island choice) 'As I Please' column whilst away on holiday. Oddly, there's no mention of this in Paul Anderson's collected edition (2006). Via Orwell, Chaplin also got in with Cyril Connolly's famous *Horizon*, though hard to think that pair had much in personal common.

'As I Please' probably inspired Chaplin to his 'Northern Accent' series for *The Guardian* – the genesis of these, with an extract from 'The Shifting Boundaries', is detailed by Richard Nelsson (*Guardian*, September 9, 2011, online). There are also palpable thematic and linguistic affinities between Chaplin's *The Cage* (1947) and chapter two of Orwell's *The Road to Wigan Pier*.

'Northern Accent' was an appropriate series title. As Richard Collis and Bill Lancaster mention in their Tyneside-focused *Roots of Regionalism* (2005, p.76), Chaplin claimed he could pinpoint specific Newcastle districts by speakers' brogue.

One oddity. According to David Kynaston's *Family Britain 1951-57*, Chaplin described the 1954 BBC production of *1984* (which I remember watching) as 'disgusting, too shocking to have broadcast'. He wasn't alone. The BBC was swamped with protests and denounced from pulpits – you can see the programme on YouTube. How would Chaplin have liked the recent local production, lavishly praised by Ken Longworth in the

Newcastle Herald (25 March 2014) under the headline '1984, Orwell's view in all its glory'?

I imagine ex-miner Ken Coates was a Chaplin fan. On a personal note, I may claim some small affinities. Just after the Second World War, I lived in the Yorkshire mining village of Dodsworth, near Barnsley, future Scargill – another Arthur! – country. Years later, I went on a school trip to Gedling Colliery in Nottinghamshire, forming the immediate impression that you can never pay miners too much.

On a different note, as a long-time contributor to *Fortean Times*, I was intrigued to read (p.143) that Chaplin was a Sci-Fi fan whose archive contains 'yellowing copies' of this magazine.

HAME provides a lavish selection of Chaplin's essays, fictions, and poems, with an introduction and eight linking commentaries by son Michael, plus a moving *Envoi*, adorned by a seventeen-page collage of colour photographs by Karen Atkinson. Elsewhere, there are several more personal black-and-white snaps. Most of the fiction concerns colliers and their lives aboveground and in the bowels of the earth. Some may think he went too often to this particular pit, but other themes supervene, my favourite – partly for personal reasons, having been a youthful deliverer of pig's fries and avid watcher of porcine slaughterings – being 'The Pig Killing'.

How to classify Chaplin's work? Obviously not Stalinist Socialist Realism. 'Social Realism' and/or 'Kitchen-Sink' make tolerable labels. Editor John Lehmann (sister Rosemary wrote her first novel in Newcastle) called it 'Pragmatic Realism'. Such distinctions easily blur. Taylor dubs it 'Working-Class Existentialism', a useful phrase in that it can mean anything you want it to.

I was much taken by the poems, not a genre readily associated with Chaplin, some of which are much in the vein of A. E. Housman, notably 'Payday':

> Twenty lads, so hearty, went down the pit
> Today.
> Twenty lads, once hearty, will never again draw
> Pay.

Also, 'Pit Pony' (p.153 - too long to quote) strikes me in its imagery as reminiscent of Chesterton's 'The Donkey'.

On the prose side, 'Letter from the Distant North' (p.243) concludes with an elegiac prophecy – now largely fulfilled – of the eventual end of coalmining as a way of life in Britain. Whether this is to be mourned or welcomed is, of course, another question.

For finale, an old joke at which I fancy Sid would have chuckled:

Snooty Woman at Reception: Oh, my husband's in oil.
Unimpressed young man: Oh, I didn't know he was a fucking sardine.

Barry Baldwin

Hell hath no fury like an author unread

James Walker (producer/editor), Paul Fillingham (art/digital producer), *Dawn of the Unread*, Spokesman/Nottingham UNESCO City of Literature, 2016, 196 pages, full colour, large format paperback ISBN 9780851248592, £14.99

When the dead go unread ... there's gonna be trouble!

Celebrating Nottingham as UNESCO City of Literature, *Dawn of the Unread* resurrects local authors and unleashes a zombie apocalypse on Nottingham's city centre in an endeavour to rescue the work of dead writers from being brushed off bookshelves and into the recycling bin. A graphic novel, *Dawn of the Unread* is the collaborative effort of more than thirty authors and illustrators culminating in the production of a vibrant collection of tales, which seek to illuminate the lives of the city's lost novelists, and many of the favourite characters from their books.

Writers such as D.H. Lawrence, Alan Sillitoe and Mary Howitt feature alongside folklore legends Ms Hood and the Gotham Fool to create individual comic strips that highlight a shared concern for declining literacy rates in Britain. The absence of a continuous plot is unimportant as the book is better designed to provide a vignette of each character's life; a snapshot, rather than an extended story. Each chapter is, however, loosely linked by the overarching theme that, if library closures continue, the authors' books would be neglected, their ideas forgotten.

Dawn of the Unread is as much a satirical commentary on twenty-first century politics and youth culture as it is a bid to educate a generation about lost literary heroes. This can most clearly be seen in the ballad of Byron Clough, fictional hybrid of local poet Lord Byron and Nottingham Forest manager Brian Clough. The poetry (by Andy Croft) conveys, with wit and guile, the importance of keeping bookshops open, whilst openly criticising the 'instant – no thinking required' way in which society has trained us to receive information. The illustrations (by Kate Ashwin) are as commendable as the written verse, since the smaller details discovered in

His hair is grey, though not with years,
His limbs are bowed, though not with toil,
His eyes are red, though not with tears,
His chamber lit by midnight oil,
A shadow of his former self –
A writer left upon the shelf.
Don Juan
BYRON
Poems About Dogs for Xmas
CLARKSON
Since books are written now by readers
Who may discover in the text
What authors (who just write the bleeders)
Do not intend, what follows next
Is that unless a book is read
It is (just like the author) dead...

My Long Walk with Slav
Script, Art, Lettering
BRICK
Colouring
Jessica Parry

MS. HOOD

WORDS: ALY STONEMAN PICTURES: AMANDA ELANOR TRIBBLE

DH LAWRENCE-
ZOMBIE
HUNTER
HUNT EMERSON & KEVIN JACKSON

the drawings contribute greatly to the overall humour of the comic.

Although entertaining, *Dawn* appears to attempt to cater for both adults and children without completely successfully managing either, leaving the reader a little unsure for which demographic the collection was intended. I cannot help but feel that the subtle comedic gibes at Tory Britain, and the general ignorance of the nation, would go over the heads of many younger readers. My assertion was tried and tested on a fifteen-year-old family member who said that she thought that she was 'missing something', mainly, the punch line. That said, the standard of prose is not consistent from chapter to chapter for a more adult audience. Although this is perhaps only to be expected in such a diverse work with so many different contributors, it often feels a little too 'textbook', and I was frequently left expecting more.

For me, the most interesting sections of *Dawn* are those when it is not repeatedly trying to emphasise library closures and their impact. At times it feels like banging a single drum, labouring the point that the majority of people generally do not read enough. Wouldn't a symphony of stories engaging the reader with more diverse plots generate a natural enthusiasm for literature, making more organic the desire to explore further?

Glimpses of such an approach do occur throughout *Dawn*, but they are rather scarce. The story of Slavomir Rawicz, 'My Long Walk with Slav', is a personal favourite that has a substantial plot whilst maintaining a level of wit and solid illustrations to match. Brick, author and artist, narrates his childhood escape from boarding school come penal institution, drawing upon Rawicz's *The Long Walk to Freedom* for inspiration. The comic is engaging and I found it much more convincing that *The Long Walk* is a worthwhile read. Similarly, the stories of Ms Hood's feminist struggle to find her way in the world, and D. H. Lawrence's rage against the capitalist machine and human 'zombies' that it created, were equally persuasive. Both comics encourage the reader to think critically about contemporary economic and political systems, adding a depth to the narrative beyond library closures and satire.

That said, regardless of the varying quality of each individual comic, *Dawn* succeeds in promoting the experimentation of different literary styles and techniques. As a result of such variety, it is possible to celebrate the rich artistic talent that Nottingham has to offer, both of the past and present-day. As a locally-minded literary work with global aspirations, *Dawn* offers something different: the opportunity to experience familiar surroundings in an entirely new way, bringing them to life, and creating a sense of excitement that can be achieved only through story-telling of this kind.

Belinda Toor

Dawn of the Unread

William Booth **Calm down it's only an Abookalypse!**
James Walker – writer, Mike White – artist, Rhianne Murphy – colourist

Slawomir Rawicz **My Long Walk with Slav**
Brick – script, art, lettering, Jessica Parry – colouring

Charlie Peace **Inside the mind of a master criminal**
Written by Michael Eaton, drawn by Eddie Campbell

The Gotham Fool **Little Boxes**
Words – Adrian Reynolds, pictures – Francis Lowe, letters – Brian Daniel

Byron Clough **'Booked'**
Words – Andy Croft, Art – Kate Ashwin

Alma Reville – Lady Hitchcock **Psychos**
Written by Nicola Monaghan, Drawn by Judit Ferencz

DH Lawrence **Zombie Hunter**
Hunt Emerson & Kevin Jackson

5th Duke of Portland **Duke and Disorderly**
Words – Andrew Mulletproof Graves, Art – Toni Radev

Bendigo **Bendigo versus Nottingham**
Words – Al Needham, Artist – Rikki Marr

Hood **Ms. Hood**
Words: Aly Stoneman, Pictures: Amanda Elenor Tribble

Geoffrey Trease **Books and Bowstrings**
Written by Alan Gibbons, Drawn by Steve Larder

Alan Sillitoe **For it was Saturday Night**
Writer: James Walker, Artist: Carol Swain

Mary Howitt **Will you walk into my parlour?**
Words: Alison Moore, Art: Corrina Rothwell

Stanley Middleton **Shelves**
Writer: David Belbin, Artist: Ella Joyce

Margaret Cavendish **Mad Madge**
Writer: Mhairi Stewart, Artist: Gary Erskine

George Africanus & George Powe **Powe meets Africanus**
Writer: Panya Banjoko, Artist: Conor Boyle

Granfalloons tumble

Brian Davey, *Credo: Economic beliefs in a world in crisis,* Feasta (publishers) Ltd., 474 pages, paperback ISBN 9780954051037, £20

At one level *Credo* is a textbook on economics, but it is a textbook with a difference. It is a work of political economy with an insightfulness that covers economics, not in the mainstream sterility of 'free markets' and 'marginal utility', but in humankind's lived experience. It encompasses lifestyle, consumerism, conceptions of nature held by indigenous peoples and, above all, our relationship with the environment and our very survival. This is also a personal work which does, to some extent, illuminate the journey of the author from the claustrophobic narrow world of Marxist groupuscules to a broader engagement with radicalism at a community, social psychological and environmental level. It is a work which complements that of Oliver James, who describes the effect of what he calls 'selfish capitalism' on the persona. Although the author may protest that his faith in a 'Marxist belief system' has been lost, it seems to me that he retains many of the insights that emanate from that source. Given this association, it is refreshing that the usual jargon utilised for such discussions has largely been dispensed with.

The first part of *Credo* (in which there are eight parts and fifty chapters) explains 'faith' as defined by the author. For him 'faith' is how we view the world, and how we reach a certain personal view which can be full of twists and turns, but essentially provides a purpose for existence. The author perhaps does not put sufficient stress on the fact that this personal 'faith' may fluctuate necessarily with our relative position in society. For example, the elite know what they want, but realise that they must retain a modicum of popular support to continue their financial and political aggrandisement. The rest of society, awkwardly, does not have just one 'faith' but, over the last 30 years, has been force-fed a model of national and international economy as something akin to household economics, with the added obfuscation of the voodoo world of high finance, far too difficult for us mere mortals to understand. *Credo* draws attention to the role of economists as a support system enabling the elite, through their pliant associates in the media, to tackle most problems on the basis that 'there is no alternative' (TINA).

In a chapter sub-headed 'Economists are a part of the elite', Brian Davey takes us down the historical path leading to present-day neoliberalism, the dominant economic 'faith'. This can be seen in a simplified form with a quotation from Anaïs Nin: 'we do not see things as they are, we see things as we are'. By way of illustration, Davey writes about the ongoing civil war in Syria as informed by the mass media, which never mentions the salient underpinning reasons for the conflict. Part One takes us on a journey through economic theory from Aristotle to the present day market-fixated economics via Ricardo, Bentham, Darwin and others. There is a lot of interesting analysis of the subjective nature of consumer choice which invalidates the current market ideology, preoccupied as it is with its pursuit of 'marginal utility' and other phantoms of the perfectly competitive market.

Davey notes the effects of colonialism and the way that indigenous peoples' knowledge and attitudes to the natural environment were largely ignored and ridden roughshod over, and in some cases they were subjected to the ultimate crime of genocide. With the 'greenwash' peeled away, we can discern a rapacious capitalism that sees the natural world as something only to exploit, often ignoring the harm done to the environment and the pollution caused. These often vitally important features of capitalism's unrelenting growth are cloaked by the euphemism 'externalities'. So, for example, the decision of the UK government to allow 'fracking' has been condemned by the two major environmental organisations, Greenpeace and Friends of the Earth, to no avail. But a cursory effort to look up fracking on the internet reveals that the world of commercial public relations has been hard at work trying to calm the worries of the public with suitably soothing weasel words.

Credo is extensive with some 400 pages, and it is not possible to give an adequate representation of all the many questions it seeks to answer, but here are a few to whet your appetite: topics such as land and nature, paid work, households and lifestyles, the unpaid work sector, entrepreneurs (social and anti-social), money and finance, credit, and politics. These indicate the work's breadth and scope. There is, for example, an extensive discussion about the two mechanisms that put the energy flow, in the advanced world, in jeopardy. The reason is that as sources of fossil fuels begin to decline their price is bound to increase, thus affecting the flow of funds to the financial system. As the reserves of oil in particular become depleted and more and more difficult to get at, the costs of actual drilling necessarily cause the price to rise, which in turn raises transportation and refining costs, forming a self- perpetuating inflationary circle. In 1972, the Club of Rome commissioned a report from the Massachusetts Institute of Technology (MIT) on whether or not the world economy could keep on growing exponentially. Their findings were published in a book entitled *The Limits to Growth* and, as Davey remarks, it is interesting to compare their assertions with what has transpired and what seems likely to develop in the future. They stated that, by 2015, the general onset of economic collapse would begin with a *per capita* fall in industrial output, by 2020 the death rate would increase, and by 2030 world population would start to fall. These latter two predictions are the result of poor nutrition and the failure of research to come up with new drugs capable of fighting new strains of diseases, when existing antibiotics have been overused and bacteria have mutated to become resistant to them.

Many of the technologies that purportedly mitigate the problems usually associated with energy production are subjected to detailed analysis and, in this context, Davey uses the term 'Granfalloons', invented and defined by the writer Kurt Vonnegut as 'a specious belief system that brings people together'. Davey notes that this is a more than adequate description for the likes of Monsanto, Proctor and Gamble, Chevron and BASF, who try to re-brand themselves as part of the 'green economy' when, in fact, they are draining other resources in the 'bio-economy'.

Thankfully, *Credo* is not without its lighter asides, for example when Davey criticises his fellow economists for judging the seriousness of a work by the number of graphs contained therein. He regales us with a tale of when the Chancellor of the Exchequer, Gordon Brown, was asked who was the most powerful person in the UK — the answer was not his leader and Prime Minister, Tony Blair, but Lord Browne, at the time chief executive officer of BP. As someone who completed a course on economics, I was happy to see the author describe the demand curve in a perfectly competitive market as 'obviously theological drivel'. Continuing from this, the effort of mainstream academic economists to make economics into a science, objectively detached from the political and social milieu that surrounds it, conveniently absolves mainstream economics from its responsibilities to society in general. For example, the ever-present compulsion to curtail government spending at all costs, based on theories related to the causes of inflation, has contributed to the worldwide development of huge disparities in wealth.

The final section of *Credo* lists some of the possibilities for staving off climate collapse, if we manage to render redundant the nuclear threat, by building a society based on human-sized small-scale units within a co-operative framework. It will not be an easy struggle, and Davey ends the book, not with the above nuclear scenario, but with a fearful thought that it might already be too late. The choice is summed up for this reviewer by Rosa Luxemburg's dichotomy, 'socialism or barbarism'.

What use could be made of this fascinating book? It is certainly one that should be given as an initial text to all those studying the areas that *Credo* focuses on, but it is a text that should bring, as I think the author desires, an ideological alignment between the environmental and labour/socialist movements. I am sure that Brian Davey's diligence in assembling and writing such a book will spark interest in many readers to investigate further the vital matters raised.

John Daniels

Land o' the Leal

Fred Bower, edited by Ron Noon with Sam Davies, *Rolling Stonemason: An Autobiography*, Merlin Press, 2015, 176 pages, paperback ISBN 9780850366242, £12.95

The introduction to this edition rather loftily cites a reviewer of the *Daily Express* when this book first came out in 1936, 'revealing as much about his class prejudices as his literary credentials':

> '… to be honest, I found it almost wholly uninteresting. I will not subscribe to the modern cant which pretends that a man has only got to be a railway porter or other wage-slave to be a master of literary fascination. A dull book is a dull book whoever writes it.'

I don't know what it says about my own class prejudices or literary credentials, but Fred Bower was a hobo stonemason who wrote a very dull book. True, he met Upton Sinclair trying to put a heavily censored version of his novel *The Jungle* on to the stage, and some of the Pankhursts, and he took a brave stand as a conscientious objector during the First World War, but this is all done in a page or two. He was a rolling stone, a hobo, a rebel with a cause (socialism), but the book reads more like a list of his endless jaunts; criss-crossing the Atlantic, up and down the UK, once to Australia. We learn very little about what stonemasonry involves, or socialism, for that matter, except bringing the Kingdom of God (good) – he always puts it in brackets – to Earth and the endless street corners and halls where he preached. We learn very little about him as a man, except that he was a heavy drinker. (Did that make him good company or a crashing bore?) Apart from a piece of doggerel to a girl, there is not a whisper of a 'private life', i.e. sex, love, marriage, kids, open relationships or gay relationships, one, some or all of which play a large part in the lives of most of us.

For a truer account of socialism, and living with or without it, you would do far better to turn to a fictional account, to a novel also published long ago in 1939 and reprinted in 1987: James Barke's *The Land of the Leal.** This massive but very readable work covers three generations of Scottish frameworkers, concentrating on the lives of a couple of the second generation from cradle to grave. The story begins in Galloway, South West Scotland. It is beautiful country with its lochs, rivers, hills and seashore (sadly, these days, somewhat contaminated by radioactivity drifting up on currents from Windscale-Sellafield). There is a love for the land but there is nothing remotely romantic about it. The work is ceaseless, grinding toil, living conditions usually awful, and the poverty is extreme. The husband has a great sense of social (in)justice but no political awareness. His wife is like a tigress defending her cubs. She defies anything or anyone who threatens a roof over the family's head or putting food on the table. Thus, when her husband leads a strike without really meaning to, one harvest time, she berates him for a fool: he will get the sack, where will they go? What will they do for food? They just get away with it as the wife gets on well with the factor, and she is a superb milker who makes the best cheese and butter for miles around. The Lady of the House (the gentry do not come out well) appreciates this, and doesn't want to lose her. But, the husband is exiled from the other men, becoming a rather degraded odd-job man.

Like millions the world over, the family is forced from the country into the city (Glasgow), where the husband obtains a poorly paid job in the shipyards. Work is plentiful during the First World War, but recession sets in later and he finds himself without work. He tramps the Glasgow streets for months. Starvation and being thrown out of house and home stare the family in the face. In the end he does find work, only to find himself ordered out on strike. No doubt, remembering his wife's former bitter recriminations and realising just how badly they need the few coppers he now earns, he refuses. Blackleg and scab. He has no time for all the -isms: socialism, fascism, communism, bolshevism, feminism.

However, the family is growing up: one wee daughter dies of diphtheria in infancy, the oldest daughter goes off to India as a nursemaid, and another decides, with her husband, to try for a better life in America. That leaves two brothers, one of whom is a committed socialist and who is killed in his first week at the front in Spain. One brother remains, the only one to be formally educated, becoming a minister. His mother has always been convinced that education is the only hope, the only way out of a life of toil and poverty, but this produces tensions, too, especially between him and his socialist brother. One thinks 'book-learning' is not really work and the other sees it as an entry to a better social class where one doesn't have to stoop so low as to soil one's hands, where bridge and golf are the order of the day. But the minister quickly becomes disillusioned with the bourgeois way of life and is reconciled with his brother before he goes off to die in Spain. The minister never surrenders his beliefs to his brothers 'atheistical and socialist' views but becomes a 'radical Christian', yet it is not a happy ending. Their father is killed in an accident, leaving their mother a lonely, exhausted woman. But the novel speaks a truth about the personal and political that Fred Bower's autobiography cannot touch.

If you want to try something a little less heavy you could do worse than watch the film *The Admirable Crichton* (1957) starring Kenneth More, Diane Cilento, Cecil Parker and Sally Anne Howes, directed by Lewis Gilbert, from the play by J. M. Barrie.

'Socialism' is not mentioned once but socialists should take note that it is films like this which will convert people to their cause sooner than many of their more formal works, which so easily send people to sleep.

A posh, aristocratic family along with their butler are shipwrecked on a deserted island. The pathetic and pampered family are in despair. All is lost but the butler, the Admirable Crichton of the title, is capable of much more than ironing *The Times* or bringing their Lord and Ladyships tea in bed. He is a 'real working man': he sets about lighting a fire, building a rudimentary shelter and finding food, and teaches his spoiled charges (he is now the boss) to do the same. He becomes a very benevolent dictator, much respected by the aristocrats, and their island becomes a kind of rustic paradise. And then they are rescued …

The lower the caste or class, the more badly paid, the more important the work usually is, whereas the higher the caste or class and the higher the pay, the more socially useless the work is. Seems a fair enough equation to me. Have you ever met a 'professional' who didn't think he or she was entitled to a higher status and pay because they had studied and passed exams? Those who have been to university know what a tough life it is, and the finals are even grimmer than working down the mines or laying bricks all day, right? I remember reviewing a book about Bevin's Boys for *The Spokesman 118* and concluding that I would have rather taken my chances storming up the beaches of Normandy than working down the mines as a Bevin Boy. The film illustrates all this admirably; as admirably as the Admirable Crichton.

Nigel Potter

**James Barke,* The Land of the Leal*, Collins, 1939, reprinted by Cannongate books, 1987, 616 pages, paperback ISBN 9780862411428, £15*